I Can't Stop -

The Gasman's Coming

by

Douglas Arthur

Best Wishes

Doug Arthur

First Published 2008 by Countyvise Limited
14 Appin Road, Birkenhead, Wirral CH41 9HH.

Copyright © 2008 Douglas Arthur

The right of Douglas Arthur to be identified as the author of this work has been asserted by
him in accordance with the Copyright, Design and Patents Act 1988.

British Library Cataloguing in Publication Data.
A catalogue record for this book is available from the British Library.

ISBN 978 1 906823 02 3

Also by Douglas Arthur:

Desert Watch – The first wagging of a Desert Rat's tail.

Forty Men – Eight Horses – The demise of a Liverpool Territorial Regiment and incarceration in a German Stalag.

*This book is dedicated
to the memory of my mother*

Contents

Chapter 1

1920 to 1929 - 45 Waltham Road

Still half asleep I found myself standing at the top of the stairs in the semi-darkness of the narrow landing, one hand holding the tail of my shirt bunched above my belly-button, the other clutching at the knob on the top of the newel post. My toes were hooked, firmly, around the stair tread, like a parrot on a perch.

"I can't stop, I can't stop", I squawked, tears of anguish and mortification running down my cheeks.

"I can't stop, I can't stop".

Like the boy statue, I was producing a steady stream of pale amber pee from my infantile penis, which fell in the graceful arc of a rainbow and spattered in tinkling puddles on the linoleum-covered stairs. Amid wisps of steam the steady, full flow glistened in the glow of the gaslight from the ceiling of the kitchen at the foot of the stairs. The incandescent light was "on the blink"; flickering unsteadily, indicating to me, even at the tender age of three, that another penny was wanted in 'the gas'.

"I can't stop, I can't - - -"

My tearful wailing ceased abruptly and I broke into a puzzled grin when I became aware that my mother and father, their faces lit up with broad smiles, and my older brothers Alf, Harold and Ken, laughing their heads off, were standing in a group at the bottom of the stairs looking up at me.

I quite failed to see the joke, but realizing the

laughter was somehow connected to the glistening arc, my bewilderment eased. The flow slowly subsided to a trickle, splashing on my bare feet, as my bladder voided. The rainbow vanished.

"It's all right, Doug, it's all right. Don't worry", my mother said, in the reassuring way of most mothers, as she made her way up the stairs. She gathered me in her arms, at the same time saying over her shoulder, "Put another penny in the meter, Alf. You'll find one on the mantelpiece. And Ken, give over laughing, and go and get the mop from the back-kitchen".

Still laughing, Alf was already on his way to the gas meter in the vestibule at the front door. Alf was accustomed to the penny 'dropping' in the meter, and the gaslight failing at inopportune moments. In fact he could find the meter, put a penny in the slot and turn the key in total darkness. More often than not, the coin came out of his pocket, too.

"Oh, good lad, Doug. You haven't wet the bed, then", mother said, as the flickering steadied, and the living room below brightened. "I'll not have to change the sheets. "

"And your shirt's still dry," she went on, "That's a good lad."

Carrying me into the smaller of the two bedrooms and squeezing past the double bed which almost filled the tiny room, she put me back in the single bed beneath the frost speckled window, tucked the sheet and blanket under my chin and pulled over my shoulder father's old Army British Warm, a relic of the First World War, now doubling up as a duvet or bedspread.

I slept, with Alf, the first born of the Arthur family, in the smaller of the two beds almost filling the tiny room. Harold, Ken, and Wally slept in the double bed, one at the bottom and two at the top. It was freezing hard, outside, and only a degree or two above freezing in the bedroom. A full moon shining through the draughty casement window illuminated, brilliantly, the frosted patterns on the glass and the rough outline of the Union Jack with the initials KGA, which Ken had scratched on the frost with his fingernail while he was waiting for me to go to sleep last night. I was tempted to climb out of my warm cocoon and try my artistic efforts on the frosted glass. Instead, I opted to blow clouds of steam from my mouth on to the window, adding to the moonlit patterns. I wondered when Alf would be coming to bed. It was always warmer when he was in the bed and he kept his socks on too.

+++++++++++++++++

With the assistance of a neighbour, "Mrs. A", (Mrs. Armstrong, the local unofficial, free-lance midwife) I was born on the 22nd of June, 1920 at 45 Waltham Road, Anfield, Liverpool, 4, the fourth son of Robert and Bessie Arthur. Dr. Bogle had made a brief appearance with his little black bag to check that everything was going along nicely before departing with his two and sixpence.

My older brothers were Alfred Edward, (Alf), then aged ten, Harold Milward, (Hal) eight, and Kenneth George (Ken), five. Walter (Wally) was born fifteen months later and I was to learn that a girl had been stillborn to my mother, in the five year gap between me and Ken, The first of my four sisters, Irene (Rene) and Jean were also born in Waltham Road, in 1925 and 1927. Making a total of nine people living, at that time, in the little two-bed-roomed terraced house.

Waltham Road, in the Cabbage Hall area of Anfield, Liverpool, was one of the countless roads containing rows and rows of identical terraced houses built all over the country. It was the first of a series of roads off Townsend Lane, magnificently named after the grand and glorious manor houses of the England of old. Waltham Road, Winchester Road, Clarendon Road, Claude Road, Lampeter Road, and Empress Road. Beyond Empress Road lay Townsend Lane Elementary School, Breck Park Greyhound Racing Track and, adjoining Breck Park

Railway Station, the railway sidings and coal depot. Townsend Lane School, with its corrugated iron roof was known as the "Tin School". The granite sets of these narrow roads terminated at the somewhat grander houses of Suburban Road, the back doors of which overlooked the playing fields of Breck Park and its bowling greens and tennis courts.

As a child the names fascinated me, as did the names of the roads on the opposite side of Townsend Lane. Priory Road, Abbey Road, Cathedral Road, Chapel Road, Monastery Road, Bishop Road, Canon Road, Vicar Road, Rector Road and Curate Road. They were all to become very familiar, later, when I delivered newspapers.

The quality, and size, of the dwellings of the "Church" roads, seemed to be graded in order of seniority of the clergymen of the Church. The imposing four-storied, semi-detached houses of Priory Road were crowned with huge, castellated chimney pots perched on twisted redbrick chimney stacks; and black painted iron railings, with fleurs-de-lis emblems picked out in gold paint, surrounded the well-kept front gardens. But the front doors of the lowly, two-up-two-down, back-to-back terraces of Curate Road, at the bottom end of Townsend Lane, opened directly onto a narrow pavement, the paving slabs of which were cracked and uneven. Strange, also, that the sole place of worship in this ecclesiastically named community was a tiny evangelical, or Salvation Army chapel on the corner of Vicar Road.

The Arthur residence, Number 45, was the end house in Waltham Road and furthest from the main road. A terraced house, with two small bedrooms upstairs, and on the ground floor, a parlour or sitting room, a living room or kitchen, and a back kitchen or scullery. There was a tiny garden in the front and at the back a long yard surrounded by high walls to the back entry and containing the outside privy or lavatory.

Although within easy walking distance of the shops lining each side of busy, bustling Townsend Lane, it was almost out of earshot of the deafening clatter and rattle of the 'bone shakers', the ramshackle, electric trams careering up and down the single tram-track. Almost, but not quite, for when I lay awake in bed in the early evening, the distinctive whine of the trams' four iron-shod wheels could be heard clearly as they rolled along the steel tramlines, oscillating crazily from side to side.

Fronting the little two-up-and-two-down dwelling was the garden. Not well manicured, like the gardens of Priory Road, nevertheless the tiny patch of hard, clayey soil, blackened with the smoke and soot of ages belching from countless chimneys, was "the garden". Behind the low brick wall at the pavement edge, an untidy, grimy privet hedge, in need of the annual visit of the itinerant hedge-clipper, struggled to earn a living for itself. The sooty hedge also doubled as a party fence between our house, Number 45, and 43, next door.

Red quarry tiles, brushed and mopped clean every day by my mother formed a neat path to the white holystoned step and, under the door, a highly polished, rounded, brass doorstep. A black, iron boot-scraper was set into the tiles on one side. "Did you scrape the mud off your boots before you came in?", mother always said. As you walked up the path you couldn't miss seeing the black enamelled figures **45**, in the centre of the half-round glass fanlight over the door. To the left of the door, a hefty, sandstone sill and lintel, painted a red gloss to match the tiled path, framed the bay window of the parlour. Crisp white net curtains, changed every week, hung in the window, hiding the emptiness of the room from the passer-by. To the right of the door, a high entry wall formed the "back-jigger" or back-entry, separating Waltham Road from the back doors of Suburban Road.

The heavy, panelled front door, and its imposing polished brass letter box and door-knocker, opened into a four-foot square lobby - the vestibule - and an amazingly colourful vestibule door, in front of which was a thick coconut-fibre mat almost covering the floor of the lobby.

In the corner alongside the front door was a penny-in-the-slot gas meter, a grey lead pipe curving out of the top and disappearing into the wall. Black letters on a round label stuck on the front of the meter proclaimed "Property of The Liverpool Gas Company".

The glass centre-piece of the stained and polished vestibule door depicted a three-decker glass galleon, with all sails set, ploughing its way through green, storm-lashed seas into a vivid sun setting in a red ball below the horizon. Framing the leaded-light pictorial seascape were matching dark red and bottle green glass panels. On hot, sunny, summer evenings, when the front door was left open to let a draught of cooling air through the house, the sun's rays, beaming over the houses on the opposite side of the road, angled through the pictorial vestibule door to swamp the parlour with a rich, soft glow, enhanced by a fascinating, shimmering curtain of red and green dust motes.

"Dancing Fairies" Mother called the glittering sunbeams. "They'll bring you good luck, Doug, they'll bring you good luck". And they did.

Chapter 2

A Sight For Sore Eyes

The colourful vestibule door opened into the parlour - "The Front Room". The parlour was empty of furniture, except for an evergreen aspidistra plant – mother's pride and joy – standing on a rickety, bamboo, bow-legged occasional table in the alcove of the net-curtained bay window. The broad, shiny, dark green leaves of the aspidistra, growing from a hefty, blue and white glazed bulbous pot, were polished regularly by my mother. There was never any other furniture in the parlour, or a fire to brighten the tiny, black iron fireplace on the inner wall. Generally used as a playroom, many noisy, thrilling adventures of Cowboys and Indians, with make-believe stagecoaches fashioned from the upturned bentwood chairs of the adjoining kitchen, were enacted in the Front Room by me, and my brother, Wally.

A few short steps across the empty room, and you were in the Living Room, or kitchen, a hive of activity from six in the morning until eleven at night.

Some twelve feet by twelve feet square, the kitchen was the focal point and meeting place for all the family; and for neighbours borrowing cups of sugar or a penny for the gas, and for Sunday visits from Uncle Pete - Mum's brother - Aunty Gertie and our three cousins, Raymond, Cecil and Winnie Sheel, and occasional, afternoon visits from Mum's Mother, Granny Sheel.

13

It was also the dining room and living room and sitting room; the conference room and reading room; the room where you did your homework or filled in your Littlewoods' Pools Coupon and where father and my older brothers argued about the likelihood of Liverpool and Everton winning next Saturday. On Sunday mornings it became the bathroom, and on Mondays the laundry room/cum drying room. And on cold, dark winter Sundays, after tea, the fire banked up with a bucketful of coal, it became the card-room where we all learned to play Newmarket and rummy and solo whist.

Taking up almost the whole of one corner, in pride of place by the fire, was an imitation-leather armchair. It had 243 brass-headed, domed upholstery tacks nailed along the arms and top of the chair. I know there were 243 because I counted them many times even before I had started school. Every evening, Father, the supreme head of the household, reclined in the armchair, legs stretched out to catch the heat from the fire in the grate, the headphones of his crystal wireless set clamped over his ears, and a "Capstan Full Strength" cigarette drooping from his lips. To the great amusement of the family, every time he moved, or crossed his legs the old leather chair emitted a rude noise. They wanted to know if it was the cats-whiskers in the wireless set. Behind his chair was a curtained sash window, looking out onto the backyard and the party wall separating our house, No. 45 from the Jones', No. 43.

The wainscoting of the walls, beneath a wooden horizontal furniture rail running around the room, was papered with an embossed Anaglypta wallpaper painted a dark green. Above the rail, on a flower-patterned wallpaper, roses and carnations, in alternate symmetrical lines, angled their way to a picture rail just beneath the ceiling. On the wall opposite the old chair, hanging from the picture rail by brass chains, were two large prints in glass frames. "When did you last see your Father" and "The Laughing Cavalier" by courtesy of W. D. & H. O. Wills and umpteen coupons collected from dad's numerous packets of Capstan Full Strength. Spaced between the pictures was a carved, wooden pipe rack holding his three pipes, usually with half-smoked tobacco still in them, as really, he was a slave to the cigarettes. Alongside hung a wooden, shield-shaped plaque, with a small oval mirror set in the top and three brushes hanging from hooks underneath; an oval hairbrush, a clothes brush and a very special brush only used by father, to brush invisible specks off his bowler hat.

All domestic and social life was carried out in this little room, in front of a black enamelled coal-burning "Combination Grate and Range". With built-in store cupboards fitted into the recess of the chimneybreast at each side, the range occupied the whole of one wall and reached almost up to the ceiling. The open, coal fire, in the well of the grate, was the sole means of heating and cooking in 45 Waltham Road. And the fire burned day and night, winter and summer, autumn and spring, heat wave or snowstorm.

A large, black iron kettle stood permanently on one of two swivel hobs, or trivets, fixed each side of the horizontal bars of the open fire. Inside the soot-encrusted kettle rolled a small, round granite or marble stone - an 'ollie', as it was known in Liverpool. A device used to attract the lime and calcium in the hard water and prevent the inside of the kettle from becoming encrusted with limescale. Periodically, it was taken out and scraped and cleaned, or replaced with a new ollie. Every once in a while the ollie disappeared, mysteriously. I was to find out that Ken had appropriated it after he had lost all of his ollies in an ollies game in the back entry.

15

The other hob was the permanent resting place of an enormous, long-handled iron saucepan. A sight for sore eyes in the icy, frost-bitten winter months of those days, was to arrive home from school to find the magic cauldron brimful with a heart-warming, belly-filling, aromatic, bubbling broth of thick, ham-and-pea soup made from a pennyworth of potherbs and a threepenny ham-shank and put on the fire by my mother to simmer away all afternoon.

To the left of the open fire, set in the range, was a cavernous oven, where mother, once a week, miraculously baked mouth-watering crusty bread in blackened, steel baking tins together with trays of delicious, golden brown, triangular potato cakes. We ate these mouth-watering, tongue-burning "winter-warmers" straight from the oven, plastered with butter and sprinkled liberally with salt, and sometimes accompanied by enormous halves of buttered, baked potato with crisped, brown skins and topped with baked beans or very strong red Canadian cheese.

They were not the only "winter warmers" to come from the old range. Every Sunday at one-o'clock, mother spirited from the oven magical "Sunday Dinners" of roast beef and Yorkshire pudding or roast pork with sage-and-onion stuffing, apple sauce and roast potatoes. Her culinary piece de resistance, however, regularly produced from this ancient appliance, were the never-to-be-forgotten, lightly spiced, brown-glazed, fruit bun-loaves loaded with currants, sultanas, raisins and candied peel. These fruit-laden masterpieces always made a regular appearance a week or two before Christmas. Many years later I had the honour of treating the members of my gun-crew with a glorious morsel of one these bun-loaves after it had found its perilous way to me across the war-torn world during my half-starved, enforced sojourn in the middle of the Libyan Desert.

One dark night in the middle of a freezing cold winter, Mother almost baked "Ginger" the family cat when she closed and latched the heavy steel door of the oven on going to bed. Our ginger-tom had, earlier, crept through the open door to sleep in the warmth of the oven, alongside two bundles of firewood left to dry and bring to life the dormant fire the following morning. Luckily mother had followed her usual practice of "damping-down" the fire with wet tea-leaves from the tea-pot, and vegetable peelings, so the ginger moggy survived the roasting.

Winter and summer, heat wave or hailstorm, snow or rain, she coaxed the fire into life at half-past six every morning; at the same time, telling the still comatose occupants of the two bedrooms above that it was time to be out of bed for work or school. The ghostly night-sounds of the humming and squeaking of slow-burning tea-leaves and vegetable parings on the fire were drowned by her vigorous application of a long brass-handled poker through the horizontal bars of the fire, raking the ashes into the basket below before shovelling them into a bucket to take down the yard to the dust bin set into the outside wall of the entry. The violent scraping of iron on iron could be heard all over the tiny house and could even be heard next door. And half an hour later we could hear Mrs. Jones, in No. 43, carrying out the same chore.

After carefully separating the still warm and burnable cinders from the ash and putting them back into the fire well, she would lay newspaper on top and then two or three sticks from the bundle of bone-dry firewood in the oven. More often than not, though, the luxury of firewood was not available so she used tightly rolled up newspaper instead. After carefully placing fresh coals on top she would put a match to the paper. In the middle of winter, very often with a foot of snow on the ground outside, it was essential that some warmth should be introduced to the

17

house as soon as possible. So to assist the flames into life she formed a 'blower' by balancing the coal shovel on the front bars of the fire and spreading over it a double page of yesterday's "Liverpool Echo", so forcing the draught through the bars of the fire at the bottom.

Sometimes, the paper caught fire, a brown scorch mark in the middle of the page quickly turning into flames, when quick action was taken by mother to move the shovel away from the newspaper and let the now blazing paper disappear up the chimney. And, if the chimney hadn't been swept for some time, the blazing paper would sometimes ignite the encrusted soot in the chimney. With a frightening, prolonged roar like two express trains going through Lime Street Cutting at the same time, or a thousand German bombers flying overhead to bomb Liverpool docks, the flames and smoke would belch, frighteningly, from the top of the chimney pot. If the local bobby passing by on his beat spotted the conflagration then there was a heavy knock on the front door and eventually a fine of five pounds for setting the chimney on fire.

To the right of the fire, a small built-in water container with a tiny, lever-handled brass tap, provided the only source of hot or warm water in the house – apart from the kettle on the hob - although there was never enough hot water in the little tank to wash the mountain of dishes after each meal in 45, Waltham Road.

This massive domestic heater/cooker was cleaned and polished regularly – usually by mother - with a shoe brush and black lead, vigorously applied with elbow grease. A dirty household chore sometimes carried out reluctantly by one of my elder brothers, and on one unforgettable occasion by me, when my best Sunday jersey and my hands and face received more black-lead than the range.

Capping the combination grate was a wide overhanging mantelpiece with a brass rail attached to the underside. On washdays, and sometimes for two or three days after, the rail was festooned with shirts and singlets, underpants and socks, towels and sheets, drying in the rising heat from the fire. Laundry also hung from the long, wooden staves of a clothes drier, fixed into the ceiling above the mantelpiece, suspended by iron brackets and lowered by a rope threaded through a pulley. Drying and airing the ever increasing washing for the ever increasing Arthur family was a major headache for my mother, especially as it all had to be moved from the fire before my father came home from work.

In the centre of the mantelpiece stood a three-legged Woolworths' alarm clock, flanked by two heavy, brass candlesticks each holding a stub of candle with rivulets of spent candle-grease congealing down the side. The candles were used in so called "emergencies" when the penny "ran out" of the gas meter and, for one-reason-or-another, there wasn't a penny to put in it - usually on a Thursday – the day before "payday". Prominent at each end were fifteen-inch high, polished, black-bronze, statuesque figurines of half naked, curly-haired warriors, riding magnificent horses, long, shiny manes hanging, neatly, each side of their necks. The coal-black chargers, snorting nostrils flared and mouths open revealing gleaming ivory teeth, pranced on hind legs, their front hooves pawing the air as if dancing a lively fandango. The fascinating fighters, perched bare-back on the massive steeds, balanced in one hand a slim, pointed lance with a fluttering pennant on the end of the long shaft, and with the other, brandished on high a hefty, curved scimitar.

On one side of the spotless, blue-and-white tiled hearth of the combination grate, stood the "Companion Set". This was a squat, polished brass oval bucket holding the fire irons, a brass-handled poker, a dust shovel with a stubby, worn-out dust brush, coal-tongs to retrieve red-hot cinders when they dropped from the fire onto the hearth, and a long, galvanized wire toasting fork with which I served an early apprenticeship at making toast. On the other side of the hearth stood two heavy flat irons resting on an iron stand. One of them had a little lid in the top where mother would put glowing cinders from the fire to heat the iron when she was ironing the shirts. These flat irons were also put to good use at Christmas time, cracking the rock hard brazil nuts Alf always brought home from his office at that time of the year.

The tiled hearth was surrounded by a deep, polished brass fender with a tiny, square, upholstered box at each end, one of which held the coal for the fire, and the other the firewood which were used by the smaller members of the household to keep warm by the fireside. The fender, in turn, was surrounded by a three-foot high, wire-mesh fireguard with a brass rail on the top. On washdays, the fireguard, like the rail under the mantelpiece, doubled as a clothes-dryer and was draped with underclothes and shirts and towels steaming before the fire. Washdays were not popular in Waltham Road.

A plain, scrubbed whitewood kitchen table, with four bentwood dining chairs, stood in the centre of the room, covered by a thin, red-and-yellow, gaily-patterned oilcloth. On Sundays and high-days, however, or when Uncle Peter and Aunty Gertie came for tea, the oilcloth was replaced by a gleaming, starched white damask tablecloth spread with home-made apple and rhubarb plate pies, glass jugs loaded with sticks of thick celery, bowls of long, crisp, green leaves of Cos lettuce, plates of bread and butter, and in the centre, a large, round glass fruit bowl containing the weekly trifle the custard on the top garnished with brightly coloured speckled cake decorations. Every Sunday was party time in 45, Waltham Road!!

During the dark winter months, and, indeed, on many of the dismal days of high summer, the gloomy, sunless room was permanently illuminated by a single gas mantle on the end of a pendant gas bracket, entwined with a sticky flycatcher, hanging from the centre of the ceiling. With a distinctive, plop–plop–plopping sound, the mantle was lit by putting a match, or taper to it and pulling one of the two chains dangling from the ceiling bracket. The delicate, 'Universal' gas mantles were bought from Storah's, the chandlers in Townsend Lane at the end of the road. They cost twopence each, or two for threepence-ha'penny. Made of finely meshed asbestos, and far more fragile than a new laid egg, they came in a cardboard box, two bayonet-type lugs holding each in place. I was told off, many times, by mother for jumping down from half way up the stairs and landing with a crash on the kitchen floor, the vibration causing the mantle to shatter and flutter to the floor, like tiny chicken feathers, or, worse still, disturbing the penny-in-the-slot in the gas meter, and cutting the gas off until it was replaced. Slotted on the end of the gas bracket, the mantle, with a faint but audible hiss, produced a feeble, yellowish incandescent glow, barely sufficient to read a newspaper, or do your homework.

The kitchen, however, was the only room in the house with the luxury of gaslight. When we went to bed, we undressed with the compliments of The Liverpool Gas Company, by the shadowy glow of the gaslight from the lamp in the back entry, shining across the yard and through the window. Or, on rare occasions, by the flickering light from the stub of one of the candles from the mantelpiece, balanced in a cracked saucer.

In the corner, on the wall opposite the fireplace, was

the staircase to the two bedrooms above, and the door to the back-kitchen, sometimes called the scullery, or wash-house.

Chapter 3

Wash-Day in Waltham Road

It was in the wash house that mother slaved, every Monday, loading the previous week's family washing into a round, copper wash-boiler set into a small, brick-built coal-burning furnace. Removing the heavy wooden lid, she would fill the copper with buckets of water drawn from a brass, cold-water tap – the only source of water in the house - fixed over a shallow, dark-brown, salt-glazed sink in the corner, underneath the back yard window. When the water boiled, she would take the lid off the top of the boiler to release a dense cloud of steam filling the tiny scullery, rivulets of water condensing on the walls and running across the floor to a grid in the middle. And then, with a "dolly peg," she would rotate the clothes, backwards and forwards, in the soapy water. This energy-sapping device was like a three-legged stool fixed on a pole with a handle at the top and manually agitated the clothes in the boiler. If this didn't remove the dirt she would bring in the galvanized bath from the wall of the yard and scrub the shirt, or Dad's grimy bib-and-brace overalls, with a hefty, stiff scrubbing brush, against a galvanised, corrugated scrubbing board.

Standing alongside the boiler was the mangle, or wringer; a contraption with two wooden rollers operated manually by turning a handle on a wheel at the side. With a pair of wooden tongs mother would drag a sheet from the boiling water in the copper and, in clouds of dense steam adding to the dripping condensation on the walls of the depressing little room, she would engage a corner of it between the two rollers, holding the sheet in position with one hand and turning the wheel to the rollers with the other. The water would be squeezed out of it to run into a bucket beneath, half of it cascading onto the quarry-tiled floor of the kitchen.

As soon as I was old enough, and tall enough, to reach the handle, I was recruited to help with the washing by turning the rollers of the mangle. With many sharp reminders to "mind your fingers in the rollers, or you won't be able to eat your dinner".

It was about that time, too, that Mother decided to try using the public wash-house in Netherfield Road and recruited me to help her carry the washing. She carried the family's soiled linen, bagged in a pillowcase, and I carried the soap and scrubbing brush in a paper bag. We caught the No.13 tram from Cabbage Hall to Everton Road, an uncomfortable journey for me, sitting on Mum's lap to save the fare, with my feet dangling over the bag of washing. We walked the rest of the way to the washhouse on Netherfield Road. A visit I was accustomed to, however, for I often went with her on a Friday evening, after Father came home with his wages, to buy groceries and meat at the cut-price shops on Netherfield Road or Great Homer Street.

My memories are somewhat vague about the washhouse but I know I didn't take to the place after the few visits I made there for the damp, and the steam, and the water condensing on the walls, and the atmosphere generally, was a lot worse than our scullery. I, of course, didn't realize that most of the women using the washhouse did not have the luxury of the use of a scullery. Thankfully, visits to the washhouse ceased when we moved to a Corporation house and Mother became the proud owner of a 10 gallon galvanized gas washing boiler with the unheard of luxury of a small hand wringer set in the lid.

Washing the clothes, of course, was only a small part of the washday drudge for mother. Laundry had to be dried, ironed and aired. In summer a reasonably easy job, for on sunny days the washing could be pegged out to part dry on a line slung out in the back yard from the kitchen to the backyard wall. In winter however, it had to be dried and aired, festooned over the furniture and fireguard in front of the fire in the kitchen, and, dripping like ancient stalactites, from the four rails of the clothes-airer suspended from the ceiling.

Mondays were dreaded in 45 Waltham Road. Particularly coming home from school on cold, wet, foggy November afternoons, to find the house dripping with condensation and laundry draped all over the place, and sometimes having to give a protesting hand with the mangle. And worse still, only bubble-and-squeak and cold trifle for tea, as the leftovers from Sunday dinner was an easy meal for mother to prepare. The only one not to complain was Mother, even though her hands were red-raw at the end of the exhausting Monday washday. Nor did father. For bubble-and-squeak was not for him. He sat down to a piece of fried, undercut steak and onions or a fillet of hake and two fresh eggs, poached in milk.

From the scullery door, two concrete steps led down to the backyard. Standing on the top step I could just about chat with Elwin or Gwynneth Jones, next door at No. 43, providing they were standing on their top step. A gap of about fifteen feet separated the scullery doors of the two houses, divided by a high brick wall, whitewashed once a year by father with a mixture of lime and whiting. "It'll brighten up the kitchen", he always said. A galvanized dust-bin was recessed into the wall next to the back-entry door at the bottom of the yard accessed through a hinged lid. It was used, mainly, to take away the ash from the fire. Almost all household rubbish was burnt, including the mounds of vegetable parings, old leather boots and shoes beyond repair, and rags and bones the rag-and-bone man wouldn't take in exchange for a goldfish. The bin was emptied once a week by the bin-man, using a special tool from the outside, to unhook it through the wall and then carrying it away on his shoulder to a horse drawn bin-wagon in the street. You could always tell when the bin-men had been because lines of fine ash dribbling from a corner of the bin left a trail on the cobbles of the entry. In wintertime the ash was spread over the sheet ice covering the cobbles of the entry.

Some of the longer backyards had been converted into little flower gardens, or vegetable plots; green, colourful oases in the endless thick jungle of brick backyards. Or, to the annoyance of immediate neighbours, a hen house had been built against the party wall, in a small area fenced off with chicken wire, to house a dozen hens and a noisy cock to wake them at daybreak. A pigeon fancier had built a wooden pigeon loft in a yard in Winchester Road and the police had to be called in because someone started to take pot-shots at the birds, with an air-rifle, as they circled the area in a wheeling, white cloud.

At the bottom of the yard was the outside water closet. There was no bathroom in the little terrace house, hence my nocturnal waterfall from the top of the stairs. The "lav" or "loo", or in Father's words, "the closet", was a whitewashed outhouse attached to the rear of the back kitchen.

It contained, high up on the wall facing the door, a massive, cast iron flushing cistern, painted a brilliant red. Embossed on the front was an image of a waterfall and the word "Niagara" and underneath "Well-Bottom Waste Preventor". A long, brass chain with a rubber ball handle dangled from an iron lever sticking out from the side, and an enormous lead flush-pipe, fixed to the brickwork with two ornate lead brackets, was attached to the outlet of the cistern. The pipe disappeared into a cane-and-white "Liverpool" hopper, or closet, set into a trap under a whitewood, plank seat fixed from wall to wall. The flushing cistern was aptly named, for, when business was

26

concluded, and with a rasping, rattle and clank the chain was pulled, three gallons of water cascaded down the flush-pipe with a steady roar like a concealed waterfall, letting everyone in the neighbourhood know you'd been to the lav. Every day, Mother scrupulously scrubbed the plain, tongue-and-grooved wooden seat, fitted from wall to wall, until the white softwood boards had been scrubbed away at the edges leaving the hard grain "rings" of the wood proud of the surface. Last week's Football Echo, cut into convenient six-inch squares, a weekly chore taught to me by Ken at a very early age, hung by a loop of string from a nail sticking out from the wall on the left.

Adjoining the lavatory, and part of the outhouse, was the coalhole or coalhouse. Once a week, usually on a Friday, the coalman delivered a bag of coal. Black of face, and covered in coal dust from head to toe, an empty coal sack pinned around his neck and hanging down his back, he shouldered a hundredweight bag of coal from his horse-and-cart at the end of the entry to the coalhouse. The bag of coal was supposed to last for a week but, in colder than usual weather, invariably it was used up by Thursday and one of the boys had to go and collect 14lbs or 28lbs of nutty slack from Wilkinsons' depot in Breck Park sidings. One of my regular chores, after school, was to fill a bucket with coal and bring it into the back-kitchen.

The only illumination in the yard came from the dim light of a square, glass-fronted Liverpool Gas Company gas-lantern fitted high up on the wall of the adjoining back entry. Its feeble light, shining over the wall, cast a daunting black shadow across the yard, and a blacker shadow in the imaginative mind of an eight year old. And even older brother, Ken, was loath to enter the dark corner at the bottom of the yard in case he bumped into "Old Nick".

The lamplighter, carrying over his shoulder a long pole with a hook on the end, had lit the gas mantles in the entries and adjoining streets, late that afternoon, followed from lamp to lamp, like the Pied Piper, by the usual noisy audience of children. Every afternoon they watched the procedure with fascination. He raised the pole and with the hook expertly opened the glass door of the lamp and pulled the little chain hanging inside. To the delight of the spectators, the three gas mantles ignited with a distinctive, plop-plop-plopping noise. On dark, November, foggy nights, however, they did little to enhance the gloom of the back entry or to light up the forbidding black shadow across the backyard and "going to the lav" was put off time and time again, until for a six-year old, it became an unavoidable adventure.

And on clear, starry, fog-free nights, the moon shone through a large, diamond-shaped ventilating hole cut in the top of the door, through which blew a blistering, icy draught almost blowing me off the lavatory seat. Sitting on the scrubbed-white wooden boards, with my trousers concertinaed around the ankles of short legs dangling over the side of the seat, all other business forgotten, I couldn't take my eyes off the slow, but sure passage of the square of moonlight on the whitewashed brick wall of the little outhouse, puzzling me why it changed shape as it moved. Much to the annoyance of Ken who had been detailed to go with me and wait whilst I performed the final ritual before being put to bed.

"Hurry up, Doug, for Christ's sake", Ken would encourage, worried by the thought of "Old Nick" lurking in the deep shadow on the other side of the yard. Sotto voice, for woe-betide him if Mother should hear the blasphemy. Although he had protested loudly at having to carry out the boring chore of "going with me to the lav", nevertheless he took the opportunity to take a sly drag on a three-a-penny Crayol cigarette. I played a juvenile joke on Ken one dark November night when I let out a screaming and a wailing for my mother, at the top of my voice, and he nearly jumped out of his skin. He opened the door as he put his fag out and said, "If you don't come, now, you young bugger, I'm going in without you".

I was soon to learn from Ken that the rainwater grid at the top of the yard, in the corner near the back door, was the urinal used most often in the winter by the five males of the household. The outside lavatory was not a pleasant place to visit on a dark, wet night in the middle of January, even when you were bursting.

Of course, there were no pos - chamber pots - except the one in my parents' bedroom, which at a very early age I had learnt to avoid. Especially when I knew my father had been to the Arkles for a pint or two and had smoked two or three Capstan Full Strength before going to sleep!

Father's chamber pot had been handed down to him from his grandfather and was considered by him to be a family heirloom and a valuable antique. No doubt if it had found its way, to-day, to the Antique Road Show this would be true, for it was a remarkable piece of glazed pottery. The large, round bowl was decorated on the outside with red and pink roses and had ornate handles, one each side, and a conical shaped cover – usually left loose on the floor alongside the po - to match. The inside was white glazed, with a mosaic of fine cracks showing signs of its great age. Its antiquity, however, didn't stop him dragging it out from its permanent parking place under the bed and filling it every night, particularly after he had had a session at the Arkles with Uncle Harry! He never emptied it the next day though. Father's piss-pot three quarters full of an odorous, dark brown liquid with the shredded remains of half-a-dozen Capstan Full Strength butt ends floating on the top, would be emptied by my Mother.

Some years later, although the Arthur Family had acquired the luxury of a Corporation House with a bathroom and separate indoor toilet, the ornately decorated chamber pot was still filled, nightly, by Father. That was until Jean, my younger sister, who, during the war had inherited the odorous task from Mother, tripped in the back yard during an air raid and Father's family heirloom was smashed into a thousand valueless pieces.

That was the story she told Father, at the time, anyway, but it came out later that she had in fact raided his tool chest and borrowed a two-pound lump hammer to do the job the Luftwaffe bombers had failed to do.

Chapter 4

The Opium Den In The Boards

There always seemed to be plenty to occupy the children of the terraces of Townsend Lane and I don't remember ever feeling bored or tired. And even after the end of a long, hot summer day when Ken had been sent to bring me in for bed, I could always find the energy to run helter-skelter from him, through The Boards and around Suburban Road, before he could catch me, protesting loudly that I didn't want to go to bed yet.

Street games were varied and plentiful and, like the seasons and the weather, came and went with the passing of the year. They were played in the street, in the back entry, or in the Boards, a plot of wasteland opposite our house, No. 45. Only extremely bad weather drove us indoors.

Little more than a brickfield, the Boards was surrounded on two sides by the back yards of houses, and on the other two sides by high advertising hoardings facing Suburban Road and the busy Lower Breck Road. The placards on the hoardings, usually painted in rainbow reds and blues and depicting happy, smiling individuals, always having a good time, never seemed to change.

Periodically, though, the brilliant pictures were renewed, and our games in the Boards would be interrupted when, with bated breath, we stopped to watch the billposter performing his free circus act on the hoardings. Positioning his ladder in the centre of the poster, and balancing precariously on one leg, he would dip a soft sweeping brush into an oblong bucket full of thick wallpaper paste hooked on a rung, below his foot. After sloshing copious amounts of paste on a section of the hoarding he would take a roll of paper from a canvas bag slung over his shoulder and magically unroll a panorama of blue sun-dimpled ocean, and with one hand, slide it into its correct jigsaw position on the hoarding. We all wanted to be billposters when we grew up!

SHARPS EATON TOFFEE

Mixed, paper-wrapped caramels spilling out of a sweets jar, and **SHARPS** the word and **EATONS** the toffee.

****

A shipwrecked sailor, with a broad grin on his face and his legs wrapped around the neck of a jar of Bovril, floating on a blue sun-speckled sea.

BOVRIL prevents that sinking feeling

****

A clothesline full of brilliant white shirts and sheets, in a flowered, sunlit garden, the long sleeves of the shirts billowing out in a gentle breeze.

RECKITTS BLUE keeps your washing white

****

A smart, uniformed Naval Officer with a heavy moustache and a trimmed, pointed beard, and bearing a remarkable likeness to King George V, superimposed against a background of a grey battleship, over the words

Players Navy Cut Full Strength Cigarettes.

10 for 6d. 20 for 1/-

****

Two scruffy urchins with dream-like expressions on their faces, drooling over a large saucepan of thick stew from which floated the smell-of-smells

AH BISTO!!!

****

There were four or five boys from the Waltham and Winchester Roads gang who, in the summer, almost every day in the Boards, emulated the antics and adventures of Just William and his gang, although they had yet to be introduced to the Just William stories. Sometimes we were raided by the Clarendon Road Bucks, a rival gang from Clarendon Road and Lampeter Road who would try to pinch our spuds when they were cooked. Occasionally these raids ended in fisticuffs, or even the throwing of stones, but were usually brought to a quick halt by an observant neighbour hanging out the washing in an adjoining backyard.

Dougie Reid was the same age as me and in my class in school. Sitting around the embers of our camp-fire in the Boards, eating half cooked baked potatoes, or sheltering from the rain in our home-made flour-sack tent, Dougie would sometimes relate to his open-mouthed audience exciting tales of derring-do in China and Japan and India. His father was a seafarer, a butcher on one of the many liners sailing out of the port of Liverpool.

"D'you know Ting Flu Lu, the Chinese Laundry on Townsend Lane?" Doug said, one sunny afternoon. "You go there don't you Doug, for your Dad's collars? Well me dad says that's an opium den. Me dad's seen 'em in Pekin'. "

We all sat up and stopped fiddling with the embers of the fire, particularly me, for I was mystified about what went on behind the sliding door in the lobby of the Chinese Laundry and sometimes let my eight-year old imagination get the better of me when I collected father's collars. Apart from the red-lettered notice over the entrance, "Chinese Laundry", there were no furnishings, decorations or pictures in the lobby of the shop. A dim electric light bulb dangling from a short length of flex in the centre of the ceiling, protected by a circle of buzzing bluebottles, did little to brighten the mysterious lobby. The only sign of anyone being at home, apart from the unusual, dampish/sweetish smell and the noisy bluebottles, was a shelf with a sliding door on the wall at the end of the corridor. There was no jangling door-bell, nor bell-push to announce my presence so I was startled when, after standing, nervously, in the eerie silence of the lobby for two or three minutes, and thinking of going back home, the sliding door was suddenly jerked back with a rattle and a scrape, to reveal, framed in the narrow opening, like the picture of the Laughing Cavalier hanging in our kitchen, the head and shoulders of Ting Flu Lu, the laundryman. Only he wasn't laughing.

Ting Flu Lu always wore the same garb every time I went for the collars. A striped tunic or shirt, fastened at the neck, with billowing sleeves reaching down to his long, thin bony hands. On his head was a sort of skullcap, or fez, with a tassel dangling from the crown to match the shirt. His narrow eyes, with lids half closed, were watering and his inscrutable face was lined, and thin, and ended in a jutting lantern jaw, long wisps of flimsy, white hair sprouting from the chin and upper lip.

He never, ever, uttered a word and on my first visit words also failed me for a minute or two. We eyed each other, silently, and he was winning the confrontation until I realized he wanted the cloakroom ticket mother had given me with the sixpence for the collars. He took the ticket and when he moved away from the window, I could see the room behind him was lined with plywood shelves and partitions each containing a brown paper wrapped parcel. He brought one of them back to the window with the other half of the cloakroom ticket pinned to it. The six collars were neatly parcelled in brown paper and tied with thin, white string and an elegant bow.

"What's an opium den, then?" Stumpy Griffiths asked, chucking another piece of old floorboard on the fire, "I've never 'eard of one of them, before".

"Eh, Stumpy, don't put wet wood on the bonny" said Les, interrupting Dougie Reid's reply. "It makes too much smoke and you'll have the scuffer around again". Les had taken a lot of time to light the fire that morning, using the glass dome-head of an old flashlamp and the rays of the sun. And the rays of the sun had been going in and out of banks of clouds scurrying across the sky and it had taken some time to ignite the damp paper. And just after he had got it going, the bobby on his Breck Road beat, had seen the smoke from the fire and made a surprise visit. So Les had to do it all over again after the bobby had gone to Wildmans for his cup of tea.

Stumpy wasn't easily taken in by Dougie Reid and could always ask the awkward question when he spun his fine tales.

"Well it's where they smoke opium, isn't it", Dougie said, impatiently, annoyed by Stumpy's stupidity but not wanting a dig in the ribs from Stumpy's stump. "Anyway, me dad sez it's an opium den, anybody should know that".

"What's opium for, then? ", asked Stumpy.

"They smoke it in a pipe," replied Dougie. "And it makes you go to sleep".

"I don't need any pipes to make me go to sleep".

"Anyway", said Dougie changing the subject again, "I bet you don't know how they get the collars so stiff and shiny? Well, they spit on 'em as they iron 'em". Me Dad told me that and he saw it in China".

"I don't believe that for a minute", Stumpy replied, scornfully. "D'you mean to tell me that they yocker on them, all day long, just to make "em shiny. They'd run out of yocker."

Still holding the platform, Dougie changed the subject yet again by saying, "No they wouldn't. But, I tell you what, 'as anyone seen any 'edge'ogs in the Boards, lately?"

Les Jones butted in, saying, "What are you asking that for, hedgehogs have got nothin' to do with spit, and collars, and the Chinese laundry".

"Well, I'll tell you," insisted Dougie, "We could make use of some of that clay at the bottom of the foxhole and make a nice tasty meal for ourselves if we had a dead 'edgehog or two."

At the mention of food we all pricked our ears up, although none of us had ever seen a hedgehog in the Boards, or anywhere else for that matter, let alone eaten one.

"'ow d'yer mean?", asked Stumpy, pugnacious derision again in his rising voice, "I've never heard of anyone eatin' 'edge'ogs before. Yer can't scoff 'edge'ogs".

"Well, you can, you see!", replied Dougie. They eat 'em in China. Me Dad's seen 'em do it, and even tasted one, once. It's easy if you have some good clay, like we've got at the bottom of the hole. You make sure the 'edgehog's dead by putting it in a bucket of water, and then you wrap it in clay and bake it for two hours in the bonny. He says the bristles come out stuck to the baked clay and the meat tastes just like chicken".

"Well you can keep it for me," said Stumpy, "I don't like chicken anyway, and before the two hours was up, we'ld 'ave the scuffer 'ere, peein' all over the 'edge'og on the bonny".

I was glad when the subject was dropped for I had never even tasted chicken, and I wasn't fussy about trying baked hedgehog either.

Dougie Reid had a fund of such strange information and never tired of relating what he called "side-splitting" jokes he had read in American comics brought home by his father from New York. And we sometimes pulled his leg when he was spinning the sea-faring tales of his father by all suddenly bursting into a chorus of "My Old Man's A Sailor", a very popular silly ditty of the day when the kids of Liverpool. It went something like this:

My old man's a sailor
'Though he's never been to sea before,
He knows about as much about the sea
As the knob on our back door.

Now he set sail
For Walton Jail
In a Black Maria van
And he got as far
As London Bridge
When the rain began to snow
As the wind set fire
To the cabin door
And the donkey wouldn't go.

Oh my old man's a sailor,
'Though he's never been to sea before,
He knows about as much about the sea
As the knob on our back door.

I was to meet Dougie again, many years later, on the occasion of my Regiment's Annual Dinner at the Broadway Social Club. He was the after-dinner guest comedian.

Stanley (Stumpy) Griffiths had been born without a left hand, (or so the story was told) which he didn't seem to miss too much. Even with only one hand he was the best peggy player in the gang and he could shin up the timber braces of the hoardings quicker than any of us. A tough little boy was Stumpy, in the summer often playing out in his bare feet. We were all slightly in awe of him, with his hard fingerless stump, which he brandished to good effect whenever he was crossed.

Les Jones (not to be confused with the Jones family next door at 43) lived in the end house in Winchester Road. His backyard door was directly opposite to ours and a violent thumping on either door, accompanied by a noise which was supposed to be the hooting of an owl, signalled a new adventure in the Boards. Les was a year or two older than the rest of us and was the natural leader of the group. He was also an expert at making steering carts out of old pram wheels and a couple of orange boxes.

+++++++++++++++++++++++++

To wander off the subject a little, as I do from time to time, Les Jones was one of the many good friends I was privileged to make during my lifetime. Inevitably, we parted company at an early age, when the Arthur family moved from Waltham Road. I did not see him again until after the war, in 1946, when we met, by accident, at the bus stop at the top of Lowerson Road on the corner of Queens Drive and Townsend Avenue. Although his face was badly scarred, I recognized him immediately, and I realized right away he had been in a "brew up", either in a tank or an aircraft. He showed no sign of recognizing me so I went over to him and said "Excuse me, aren't you Les Jones, who used to live in Winchester Road. I'm Doug Arthur from Waltham Road. You were the " horse" that pulled me up and down Suburban Road in your homemade cart. Do you remember?"

His scarred face broke into a broad grin and lit up with recognition. He replied "Yes. I do I remember it. I remember it very well".

During the course of our very brief conversation he told me that he had in fact been in the crew of a tank and had taken part, as I did, in the Battle of Beda Fomm in the Italian Campaign of North Africa early in 1941. His tank received a direct hit by a shell from an Italian field gun. Les was the only survivor, and although badly burned about the face and the upper part of his body, he hauled himself out of the tank still in one piece.

That brief meeting with Les Jones, after all those years, made my day, for his wife, obviously pleased I had recognized him, said to him, "There you are, Les, this chap hasn't seen you for sixteen years and knew you right away". As we got on the bus, in an aside, she thanked me for making myself known to him and said that he was going through a bad period of depression about his scarred face.

+++++++++++++++++++++++++

In the Boards, we taught ourselves to make tents and sleeping bags out of old flour-sacks begged, or filched from the Abbey Bakery at the end of Abbey Road and rinsed out in our wash-boiler after mother had finished her washing. We borrowed a bodkin from her sewing needles and with the thin string from the Chinese Laundry Opium Den learned how to tack the sacks together. When the Robin Hood season came along – usually when "Robin Hood and his Merry Men" was on the Saturday afternoon matinee at the Cabby - we made bows and arrows from thin bamboo canes borrowed from mother's net curtains. The pointed, lethal arrows, fledged with cigarette cards, and their points hardened in the ashes of the fire, sank an inch deep into the home-made bull drawn with coloured chalk on the back of the hoardings.

We learned how to make a fire from scraps of wood, waste paper and old rags - anything that would burn - to roast potatoes pinched from the sack outside Ashtons, the greengrocers. We only ever helped ourselves to two or three, and as the sack was in full view of Mrs Ashton, I'm sure she was aware of what we were doing. Every so often, the friendly Bobby on the daily Cabbage Hall beat – a well-known policeman in the area – would see the smoke from the fire curling over the top of the hoardings and would come in the field to investigate. He was never quick enough to catch us, though, and we would double round to Suburban Road and, through a chink in the boards, watch him scraping the ashes of the fire to see if a potato was soft enough to eat, and then, after he had eaten the charcoal covered spud, peeing on the fire to put it out before resuming his beat to cadge a cup of tea from Wildman's, the newspaper shop at the top of Suburban Road.

On cold winter days, when the ground was frozen six inches deep, we made "winter warmers" - portable fires made with discarded socks or remnants of old shirts stuffed into empty marmalade cans with holes pierced in the side. Whirled, dangerously, at arms length, by two wires attached to the top of the can, they spat out a stinking ring of spluttering sparks and sooty, black smoke.

We learned how to climb, upside down, clinging like a monkey on a stick to the underside of the timber baulks holding up the advertising hoardings, a ready made climbing frame. Stumpy, with his one arm was the best of the lot of us at shinning up the wooden brace, and how to dig a foxhole in the muddy clay and form a roof over with a couple of old flour sacks. Many years later this knowledge proved useful in the aforementioned Libyan Desert.

We made steering carts, (or rather Les did) out of discarded pram wheels and empty orange boxes and raced each other down the steep slope of traffic-free Suburban Road to crash into the railings of Breck Park at the end of Clarendon Road. As we grew older, these "steeries" became more elaborate with a passenger at the back of the driver and a "proper" steering wheel with a rope attached to the axle. Sometimes we rigged them up with a piece of a flour sack to make a sail. And, if the wind was in the right direction, sailed them along Waltham Road.

Chapter 5

Peggy, Ollies and Ciggies

And in the Boards we played Peggy and Ollies and Ciggies.

The game of Peggy, invented by the kids of Liverpool, was ideal to play in the comparative safety of the Boards. We made the peg out of a short piece of discarded broom handle, five or six inches long, tapered to a rough point at each end. The idea was to hit the tapered end on the ground with a piece of old 2" x 2", or broken floorboard and when it sprang up, usually at an angle, you had to clout it as far as you could. The winner was the one who hit the peg the furthest. A sure way of training the quickness of the eye with the reaction of the hand for budding cricket, baseball, golf or tennis players, providing you didn't get in the way of the pointed peg. On one memorable occasion, Dougie Reid clouted the peg over the backyard wall of one of the houses and broke a window, causing us to make a frantic, hurried exit through the back-entry by the Cabbage Hall Picture House. When a window was broken, there was great consternation in Waltham Road until somebody's mother stumped up the seven-and-six to replace the glass. Always followed by a docking of meagre pocket money for weeks ahead.

An even more perilous game played in the Boards was "cockshy"; throwing a flattened-out tin can a distance of about twenty yards at an empty can stood on one of the stakes holding up the boards. Great care had to be taken by the spectators to keep out of the way of the flattened can, the edges of which became sharper as the day wore on and causing the missile to fly off at any angle. A version of this ancient pastime was used by the baddy in the form of a hard bowler hat in one of the James Bond films.

Another somewhat dangerous, but hilarious pastime was "muck-o-nettles". Usually "played" against the gable end of the house on the corner of Suburban Road by a team of half-a-dozen or more boys of varying ages and sizes. Taking it in turns, one boy would lean against the wall with his arms and legs outstretched and his head down between his shoulders. Then the others, in turn, would take a running jump from the opposite side of the street to land on his back or shoulders, the rest following as quickly as they could until the whole pyramid of laughing boys collapsed in a heap. The idea was to see who was the strongest in the group and carry the weight of the most boys before collapsing. Strangely, I don't remember anybody receiving broken arms or legs. But there were many grazed knees and black eyes.

And of course, everybody collected cigarette cards, in and out of season. Most males over the age of about twelve smoked, and every packet of ten cigarettes, of whatever make, contained a beautifully illustrated, and neatly printed card. So there were plenty to go around. Nevertheless, in spite of the extensive swapping and trading of cards, or winning soiled, dog-eared specimens at games of ciggies, or ollies, it was always difficult to collect a full set of Cricketers, Footballers, Butterflies of Great Britain, Seashore Seashells, Regiments of the British Army, or whatever subject W. D. & H. O. Wills had decided to put in their packets of Capstan or Players Navy Cut. There always seemed to be one or two numbers missing, making it extremely difficult to collect a full set. Wally had the best collection of complete sets among the Waltham Road boys, and kept them in a special place in father's cupboard in the kitchen. Unfortunately, his carefully hoarded, pristine sets of cigarette cards become another casualty of the war.

Incomplete sets of cards, stored in an old shoebox and kept under the bed, were used to play various games of ciggies. Flicking a card at another card balanced against the wall on the ground was the most popular ciggies game. Taking it in turns, the one who knocked over the card against the wall won the other cards missing the target.

Ollies, however, was the most popular game of all and played all the year around   except when the ground was frozen in winter.

A simple, poor-man's game costing nothing to play, apart from a ha'penny for an ollie, and played by anyone, of any age, from about six.

Ollies was a hybrid game of unknown origin, seemingly developed over the years from a combination of crown-green bowls without the grass, French boules without the metal balls, croquet without the mallets and hoops, golf without the niblicks, and billiards without the cues or baize-lined billiard table. Apparently, only played in Liverpool, for, in later life I never met anyone who played ollies as played in the parks, open spaces, brickfields and back entries of Liverpool before the war, or had even heard of the game for that matter. Highly skilful, and not to be confused with the cissies', or girls' game of glass marbles, the game was played with sturdy, one-inch diameter marbles known as ollies, over three holes dug into the surface of a short, level pitch. Made from some sort of composition of chalk and cement, when new the ollies were highly decorated with coloured patterns and were apt to split into two halves if hit hard enough in the course of the game. Lucky was the player who acquired an extra hard ollie, difficult to crack. And woe-betide those who tried to use metal ball bearings!

There were no known written Rules for the game of Ollies, but the unwritten rules, which never varied, were very strict and always followed. The pitch could be any flattish, even surface, preferably of hard, baked clay, free of broken bricks, sundry rubbish, dog-dirt or horse droppings. But at a pinch, any surface would do - even the granite sets of the back entry, as long as you could dig three small holes in it! The holes, set about ten yards or so apart formed the targets and the basis of the game, like the holes on a golf course. The opening player would be decided by the toss of a coin, or, if a coin wasn't available - as was very often the case - a trial throw was made. The ollie nearer to the hole in the centre of the pitch had the first throw of the game.

Using the end hole as a starting point, or base, the first to play would throw, flick, or roll the ollie , aiming to drop it into the centre hole. The throw used depended on the skill or preference of the player and the condition of the pitch being played. Some threw the ollie delicately between finger and thumb, or underhand from the palm of the hand. But the popular throw was a flick of the thumb from the top of the forefinger. If it went in at the first attempt he would then carry on to the third hole on the pitch. However, if it stopped short of the hole, as it usually did, his competitor would then take his turn. The ollie nearest the hole, after the first throw, won the right to the next throw and he could choose to aim it at his opponent's ollie, attempting to knock it further away from the hole, or take a second shot at the hole. If he missed, he lost his turn. Alternative throws were played unless you holed your ollie or hit your opponent's. You then had another throw.

Three circuits up and down the pitch were played to complete the game. "Openers", the first round, followed by "segs", or second round and then "lasseys" the last round. The first to reach the final hole of the lasseys round was the winner. Rules were strict. No "pudging" (cheating), or moving the ollie nearer to the hole, on the sly when your opponent's back was turned, and no second chances were allowed. The winner received his opponent's ollie. (The prize-giving usually postponed to a later date.)

In those days of mass unemployment the game of ollies was very popular with many of the unemployed Liverpool youths attending one of the compulsory "dole schools" to qualify for their dole money - unemployment benefit. Sometimes, after their compulsory game of football on Breck Park, many of these lads played ollies, gambling for ha'pennies or pennies on the result of a game. George Green, a sports cartoonist with the Liverpool Echo in the late 1920s, occasionally featured the "dole boys" playing ollies on pitches in Breck Park or Sheil Park.

Sometimes, the dole-school youths also played the illegal, back-entry game of "Pitch and Toss" the original version of the Australian gambling game of "Two-up". As many as twenty or thirty lads would gather in a circle in the entry at the back of Clarendon Road. A couple of youths were stationed each end of the entry, keeping dowse, to warn, by a two-finger double whistle, of any approaching policeman. When the players heard the whistle they scattered in all directions, some hiding in the privet hedges and rhododendron bushes around the bowling green. To be caught by the law meant a docking of the paltry dole money.

I had had strict instructions from Mother to keep away from these illegal gatherings. But, in company with Les Jones, one afternoon, I found myself on the outskirts of a group playing the forbidden game. Les and I, completely absorbed in watching the toss of the coins and making mental guesses which side they would come down on, suddenly heard the shrill warning whistle from the boy on dowse at the corner of Clarendon Road and Townsend Lane. The pitch and toss players scattered, like Autumn leaves being blown in a gale along Lower Breck Road.

I joined in the frenzied exodus, and running down the entry caught my heel in a hole on an ollies pitch and went sprawling. I arrived home with a scrape the size of a half-crown and blood running down my leg. I got little sympathy from Mum. "I told you to keep away from those ruffians playing that game. Go and wash that knee and stay in for the rest of the day. And you're not going out tomorrow. "

Ball games were always popular but restricted by the shortage of balls. So we made "Caseys" or caseballs - the original soccer football - out of tightly rolled up newspapers tied with string, to play football. They were soon kicked to shreds on the granite sets of the back entry, as were the toecaps on our boots.

In the summer, old, threadbare tennis balls, handed down by older tennis-playing brothers or sisters, sometimes made their appearance. These were put to good use in games of cricket against stumps painted on the wall of the entry or against the green painted lamp standard at the top of Waltham Road. Games of catch-as-catch-can were played against the gable end of the wall of the house on the corner of Suburban Road and Waltham Road. A tennis ball, or a hard sorbo rubber ball was thrown against the wall at an angle, after the manner of a game of squash, the loser being the one who failed to catch the ball on its return from the wall.

Mischievous - and to us hilarious - games were devised with long lengths of black cotton, or thin string. One end was tied to a carefully wrapped empty box left on the pavement in a strategic position, at the corner of the entry and, when some dear old lady bent down to pick it up, the other end was pulled sharply by a scruffy boy lying in the mud beneath the privet hedge in the front garden. Or the cotton thread was looped through a knocker on a front door and pulled clear after the knocker was given a rat-a-tat-tat. These games sometimes ended with calamity when a neighbour caught the offenders and frog-marched them by the ears to their homes.

Chapter 6

The "Brecky"

Breck Park, in those days, was a much used and very popular playing field, situated as it was, right in the middle of the densely populated area of Cabbage Hall, Breck Road, Townsend Lane and Tuebrook. On the corner of Lower Breck Road and Suburban Road, it boasted two immaculate public bowling greens and grass tennis courts surrounded by high, neatly clipped privet hedges. And at the top of the field, alongside Lower Breck Road, a narrow grassed area with park benches and a footpath bordered with shrubs and well-laid out flower beds, was the start of a pleasant walk to one of the larger landscaped parks of Liverpool – Newsham Park.

Apart from this well tended area, Breck Park was little more than an open field. There was no boating lake or heated Palm House, grassed cricket pitches or gravelled paths, but nevertheless, the field was used extensively throughout the year, mainly for football and ollies in the winter and baseball and ollies in the summer. The Brecky was also a venue for annual shows, travelling fairs and circuses and above all, Liverpool's famous May-Day Parade.

The May-Day Parade was held on the first Saturday of May. It was a unique, spectacularly decorated procession of the horse drawn commercial traffic still being used at that time and only slowly being replaced by motor transport. Taking part were horses and ponies of all breeds and sizes immaculately groomed and preened that morning, manes and tails plaited into black, shining ropes, horse brasses and leather harnesses polished and blinking in the morning sun. They were hauling their now empty coal carts and drays and milk floats and hansom cabs, all freshly painted and gaily decorated for the occasion. A detachment of Mounted Police usually made an appearance with contingents from local Territorial Regiments in full dress uniform and fixed bayonets, or an artillery battery hauling huge, 1st World War howitzer guns.

The spectacle attracted the largest of crowds for there was no entrance fee to see the eye-dazzling parade as it assembled in the judging rings of the crowded park. And the main roads also – West Derby Road, Lower Breck Road, Breck Road and Townsend Lane – leading to the park, were lined with spectators watching the passing parade. From our vantage point in No. 45 Waltham Road, the procession almost passing our front door, the May Day Parade was a well-remembered highlight of the year.

Magnificent shire horses in teams of two, four, or even six, usually headed the procession down Suburban Road pulling clean, freshly painted coal carts decorated with garlands of rainbow-coloured paper chains and flowers. Horses which, on workdays, were an every-day sight around the docks of Liverpool, with their carts heavily laden with bales of cotton, timber, grain and all manner of produce and goods from the cargo ships unloading at the docks. And for me, a vast contrast to the coal-carts I saw every day stopping at the weighbridge at Cabbage Hall to weigh their empty carts before filling them at the coal depot at Breckside.

The May-Day Parade, too, always meant a bit of a bonus for me and Les Jones; for after the parade finished, Suburban Road was littered with heaps of steaming horse droppings, and neighbours with allotments on Coney Green, or those who had turned their back yards into miniature flower gardens or vegetable plots, were quite willing to pay us a ha'penny a bucket for the fresh manure. So our orange-box steering cart was kept very busy after the parade finished and we earned ourselves a few coppers for the next visit of Wallis' travelling fun fair.

As an added spectacular bonus for the kids, the "Illuminated Tram" made its annual appearance on Mayday. The ancient, open-topped bone-shaker was blanketed with a solid mass of multi-coloured electric light bulbs, from the cowcatchers at the front, to the trolley arm sprouting from the top deck. The unusual mobile display dazzled young eyes accustomed only to the hazy lights of street gas lamps and the yellowish half-light of a flickering living room gas pendant. In pride of place at each end of the tram, over the driver's cab, was an illuminated Liver Bird with green, spread-eagled wings and a long red beak, and both sides of the tram were embellished with a dazzling replica of the Crown of Great Britain set in the middle of a flashing red, white and blue Union Jack. As the illuminated spectacle trundled its way slowly down Breck Road, we could hear the stirring sound of Land of Hope and Glory played by the Liverpool Corporation Passenger Transport Department's brass band on the top open deck. The illuminated tram stopped at the single line at Cabbage Hall and before carrying on to Norris Green the band gave a spirited rendering of "Here Comes the Galloping Major".

Chapter 7

Baseball Or Biscuits

Breck Park, in the years between the two world wars was also the home of the game of English Baseball played in Liverpool and South Wales long before serious attempts were made to introduce the game of American Baseball to the U.K. Governed by the English Baseball Association, English baseball was a cross between the ancient game of rounders played in England since time immemorial and American Baseball, the national game of the USA. English baseball, in those days of mass unemployment, was popular in Liverpool because it was an alternative to the more expensive and exclusive cricket, tennis or golf clubs.

The rules for English baseball were much the same as the rules for rounders but the game itself was extremely aggressive and far more competitive than the girls' game. A team was made up of eleven men all batting in turn until declared out by being stumped at a base, or the ball being caught after a hit, or failing to strike after three good balls being bowled. Two innings were played and runs were scored at first, second, third and fourth base depending on the batsman's skill and guile.

The pitch comprised four bases, or posts, laid out in the shape of a diamond. The ball was bowled 'underhand' from the bowler's box to the batsman standing on a crease at a corner of the diamond. The ball was the same leather-bound hard ball of the American game but the padded leather mitts, or catcher gloves of American baseball were not worn, except by the backstop who donned thick cricket, wicket-keeper type gloves, and to protect the eyes and face, a simple, wire mask. Broken fingers and black eyes were not uncommon in the game of English baseball, and the ball becoming firmly lodged in the wire eye-slit in the back-stop's mask was an accepted risk of playing at backstop, as was the possibility of a bruised or broken rib.

The bat was the same size and width as a wedged and spliced cricket bat with a flat hitting surface, but with the shoulders shaved off from the splice to the bottom edge to form a tapered bat. The ball was bowled underhand from a six foot long by two foot wide box, to a three foot wide crease, and had to be delivered between the batsman's knee and shoulder. Three bad balls failing to make this target and the batsman had a free run to first base; and a bye was awarded if the bowler overstepped the mark in the bowler's box. Great speeds could be achieved when the ball was bowled underhand with a short run, or a hop and skip, from the bowler's box, particularly if the bowler was skilful enough to jilt or throw it underhand, as most of the top bowlers did. A good bowler would also be able to dramatically swerve the ball from right to left or put a deflecting top-spin on it.

The teams in the English Baseball Association League in Liverpool were mainly from factory social clubs keeping together their winter football teams after the soccer season ended in April and, in fact, played baseball in their winter, soccer strip. British Enka (Brenka) the silk works, Crawfords Biscuits (Crystal), The Meccano, Hartley's Jam Works (Aintree) to name a few. School or church social clubs - Oakmere, Liverpool Amateurs, Oakfield, St. Marys and St. Margarets – made up the league. In those days of high unemployment, work could be found for a good baseball player, particularly if he was a bowler, if he was out of work or looking for a better-paid job.

51

Two international baseball games played under English Baseball Association Rules were held every year between England and Wales. The international sides were made up with players from Liverpool clubs (England) and Cardiff clubs, (Wales), South Wales being the only other area in the U.K. playing baseball to English Baseball Association Rules. One game was in Cardiff and a return game in Liverpool, usually held at Breck Park. Later this venue was changed, Internationals and Cup Finals being played at the White City field – later to become White City Greyhound Track - the other side of Lower Breck Road. And there was one memorable year when the International game was held at Goodison Park, the home of Everton Football club.

There were Junior leagues, fielding teams from boys and youth clubs, for boys aged between fourteen and eighteen, and Liverpool Elementary Council Schools promoted leagues of teams for twelve to fourteen year olds, playing in the parks. I was first introduced to the game of English Baseball playing for Anfield Road School - as did my three older brothers before me - and appeared in two finals at the Police Athletic Ground, losing both to Townsend Lane School, the "Tin School". Townsend Lane School, playing on their home ground at Breck Park, always seemed to produce the best players and invariably topped the schools leagues.

To digress, again. On one occasion during my last summer at Anfield Road School, at the end of a Science Class, our renowned Science Teacher, Mr. Copestake, said to me in his usual slightly derogatory, sarcastic, tone of voice, "Arthur, you're down to play baseball to-morrow, after school, and there's a class trip to Jacobs Biscuit Factory in the afternoon. You can't do both. So what's it to be, baseball or biscuits?" Even though I knew there would be a bonus of a box of biscuits at the end of the trip, and the feint prospect of a job in Jacob's factory or office I replied firmly, "Baseball, Sir". He smirked as he threw a piece of chalk at me. "See if you can catch that then", he said.

I enjoyed many happy hours playing baseball, finding the energy, somehow, to play two innings of baseball in an inter school match after finishing school at four o'clock, and then collecting and delivering a round of Liverpool Echos between six and seven o'clock, followed by, in the long summer evenings, knocking a baseball about on Breck Park, or Clubmoor Recreation Ground until it got so dark we couldn't see the ball. In between games, Mother's gargantuan dinners satisfied my ravenous appetite until it was topped up by a late night visit to the chip shop after we finished playing.

Chapter 8

The Jiggers and Back Entries of Townsend Lane

The Jigger, a narrow passage way about four feet wide, was a short cut from half way up Waltham Road to the wider entry running between the back doors of Waltham Road and Winchester Road. The walls of the gable ends in the jigger, without windows or doors, stretched to the apex of the roof and echoed loudly the staccato, ghostly, clickety-clack, clickety-clack of my steel-tipped shoes as I ran between them. I always ran down a jigger. Never walked. But, after dark, I never ran, or walked, through the black, unlit, eerily echoing entry, much preferring to take the long way round.

The narrow jigger accessed the wider back entry, wide enough to take a horse and cart rumbling over the granite cobble stones, and was used, regularly, by itinerant privet-trimmers, knife-sharpeners, rag-and-bone men, pedlars, tinkers, fishmongers, the bread man and the Hokey-Cokey ice-cream man. Every six months or so, the jiggers and entries were visited by a team of corporation street cleaners, pushing a two wheeled handcart laden with coils of hosepipe, industrial sweeping brooms with long, ultra stiff bristles, wide shovels and other implements of the road-cleaning gang. After the loose, wind-swept debris of rubbish, fag-ends, and empty cigarette packets had been swept away the cobbles were hosed down by the hose attached to a fire-hydrant in the middle of the entry, swishing away the caked dog-dirt, chewing-gum and trails of ashes left by the bin man.

A regular visitor to the entry was Ronny the rag-and-bone man, pushing a brightly decorated, two-wheeled handcart, hired that morning for sixpence a day, from Johnny Jones and Sons, Great Homer Street, Liverpool, at least, that was what the ornate, gold painted sign on the side of the cart proclaimed. Tattered old clothes and cracked down-at-heel boots and shoes, threadbare woollen pullovers and cardigans were heaped on the cart.

Winter and summer, Ronny-the-Rag-Man wore the remnants of his calling; a threadbare, faded, ex-army khaki overcoat, minus buttons, held together with a thick piece of string wrapped around his waist. A once white silk scarf circled his neck, below his prominent Adam's apple, one end dangling down his back, the other end reaching down to his ankles at the front threatening to trip himself up. A grimy, greasy flat cap was apparently, welded to his head.

Red, blue and yellow balloons pinned to the back of the cart bobbed, gaily, up and down in the wind as he pushed the cart down the entry, calling at the top of his voice, over and over again, an unintelligible sentence but which everybody recognized as" Rags a' bones, rags a' bones, goldfish for rags a' bones"

Half way down the entry, sitting on one of the long shafts at the front of the cart, he would repeat his incomprehensible jargon until Jimmy Armstrong, his arms laden with sundry items of old clothes, or a box full of empty beer and lemonade bottles or jam jars came along. Supervised by Mrs A. standing by her back-yard door, muscled arms folded on her ample bosom, Ronnie would rummage through the proffered items and take out an empty two-pound jam-jar. Dipping it into a bucket in the well of the cart he would scoop up a tiny goldfish about two inches long, desperately swimming about with its mouth open in the jar half full of water, and give it to Jimmy.

Taking a step forward, Mrs. A, would unfold her arms and place her hands on her substantial hips, jaw thrust forward, like a heavyweight boxer, saying "They're worth at least three you mean old bugger. You'll get a penny each for them jam-jars. So give him another one or I'll take the bloody things back"

Ronnie didn't argue. He fished another tiny Golden Carp out of his bucket and put it into the jar, at the same time breaking out into his opening lament, "Rags-a-bones, rags-a-bones, goldfish-for-rags-a-bones'

Another regular visitor was the Salt-Lady with her strangely muted cries of "Penny-a-block, salt, only a penny-a-block. Saaaaaal, saaaaaal". She was a tall, handsome, fascinating figure of a woman, a real Mary-Ellen, if ever there was one. In all weathers she wore a long voluminous, and to me, mysterious, jet-black shawl, fastened with a large, bright, glistening brooch under her ample chin. It cascaded over her shoulders, like Dracula's cape, brushing the cobblestones of the entry. The polished toecaps of her heavy workman's boots peeped out from under the hem of the shawl. On her head she carried ten blocks of salt, each the size of a house brick, balanced, precariously, like the Leaning Tower of Pisa, on a cloth, turban-like arrangement in her black swept-back hair. Like the Leaning Tower, they never fell. For a penny, she would reach up to the topmost salt brick and wrap it in a sheet of newspaper miraculously produced from somewhere under her shawl. She would drop the penny into a cloth pouch tied around her ample waist.

One of my early chores for my mother, was to cut a piece off the salt block, crumble it on newspaper with the flat iron, and fill the large glass salt cellar standing in its place on the living room table. We used a lot of salt in 45, Waltham Road!

The fishmonger was another Mary Ellen. Like the salt lady, her head held high and her shoulders braced back, she would walk down the entry with a large, oval, straw basket, nestled like a black, broody hen, in the turban arrangement on her head. In the basket, she toted fillets of hake and haddock, kippers, mackerel, speckled plaice and small, flat dabs. To complete the mobile fishmonger's shop, the basket also held the tools of her trade, a tiny, black-iron weighing scale.

"Fresh fish, fresh Irish Sea fish, caught this morning, fresh as a daisy" she cried, "And the cheapest on Breck Road. "

Although Ashton's greengrocers shop was only a couple of hundred yards from our house, Mr. Ashton was also a weekly visitor to Waltham Road with Queenie, a bad tempered, pie-bald pony harnessed to a long four-wheeled cart stacked with vegetables and fruit. He always stopped his cart in the street outside No. 45 and, from the safety of the front room window, I would watch the sparks flying from Queenie's hoofs as she tossed her head wildly in the air and restively pawed the granite sets of the road. It wasn't safe for me to go out until Mr. Ashton had hitched a nosebag around the head of the snorting animal to keep her quiet. I watched her tossing the bag in the air, over her head, to release clumps of hay lodged in the bottom. I was very careful of going too close to Mr. Ashton's restive animal.

The War Veterans wandering minstrels chanted their war-songs as they limped along in the road at the front of the houses. Five old looking young disabled ex-servicemen, dressed in shabby remnants of ill-fitting uniforms of the First World War, strung across the road. In one gutter a gaunt, lanky, ex-Kingsman, minus a leg, leaned heavily on a wooden crutch under his left armpit. His empty trouser-leg, folded at what was the knee, and pinned back to his threadbare jacket, was a stark reminder of the missing limb. In his right hand he held an army cap to receive any proffered pennies or ha'pennies as he hobbled along. Next to him, his stiff leg swinging heavily sideways, as he rolled along, was a blue-suited ex-sailor, his bell-bottom trousers flapping in the breeze. He was guiding a blind man, whose outstretched hand clutched the sailor's shoulder. The other two boyish veterans had each lost an arm. The empty sleeves of their ex-Army khaki jackets dangled in the air, grotesquely, as they walked along singing 'It's a Long Way to Tipperary' or 'Keep the Home Fires Burning'. The one on the end, in the other gutter, carried a biscuit tin holding the few coppers he had collected and which he rattled in time to the rhythm of the song, as he walked along. I wondered how long it would take them to get to Tipperary.

Although often hard pressed to find a penny to put in the gas meter, Mother never failed to find a coin to put in the young veterans' collection box.

Another regular street busker was a somewhat elderly, toothless tramp with a very pale face, red gums prominent in his wide-open mouth as he sang, in a high-pitched falsetto voice with his head thrown back, the same two sentimental songs from the old Music Halls. 'It's the Ring My Mother Wore'. And 'She's Only a Bird in a Gilded Cage'. Unkindly nick-named Gummy by the kids, when he saw an adult he would doff his greasy, flat cap to reveal a completely bald head, as he held it out to receive a coin or two. Gummy, in rain or hail, also entertained the queue for the sixpennies at the first house at the Cabbage Hall Picture House and then, jumping on a tram, was just in time to catch the one-and-nines queuing for the second house at the Clubmoor Cinema in Townsend Lane.

In those days of television-less, radio-less and, for the most part gramophone-less households, the One-Man-Band, also, was an ever-popular visitor. He, somehow, managed to play, at one and the same time, a mouth-organ strapped to his shoulders in front of his mouth, a concertina swinging across his stomach and keeping time by thumping an enormous drum strapped to his back and operated by a cord tied to his left heel. Demonstrating his musical talent further, he would sometimes switch to playing a penny whistle instead of the mouth-organ.

The Piper was clad in full Scottish Highlanders

regalia, from his Glengarry bonnet and tartan ribbons down to his knee-length stockings with a dirk sticking out of the top and highly polished black boots. His tartan kilt and sporran swirled and bounced in time to his Highland lament as he marched up the middle of Waltham Road, a line of laughing children marching in step behind him.

The annual visit of the knife-sharpener to the entry, was another star attraction to the kids, always drawing alongside a crowd to watch him convert his two wheeled, sit-up-and-beg Raleigh bicycle into an efficient grinding machine, by linking the grindstone to the pedals of his cycle. Sitting on the seat of the bike, pedalling away, he would sharpen anything from a meat carver to a set of old wood chisels. As he turned the twelve-inch circular grindstone the sparks flew from the carving knives and cutlery of Waltham Road, like a Catherine Wheel on Guy Fawkes' night.

Gus, the "Echo-lad" was a daily visitor – or I should say early evening visitor – selling his newspapers in the roads off Townsend Lane. We could hear his gravelly voice shouting his unintelligible cries long before he trotted into Waltham Road from the main road.

"Last City Echo, City Echo, Liverpool Echo, Last City Echo". Or, "Express, Evening Express. All the latest on the Wallace murder case. Evening Express". That's what he was actually calling, but, in fact his voice sounded more like a hoarse Swiss yodeller and only the mature and experienced, like my Mum and Dad, could interpret the high-pitched phrase. On Saturdays, Dad, anxious to check his football pools coupon – the "Pools" had just made their appearance at about that time - would hand me a penny, saying, "There's Gus, Doug, go and get the Football Echo, Make sure it's got the results in. "

Gus was a stocky, thickset man with a distinctive thatch of carroty red hair, badly in need of a visit to a barber, and a florid, open-air complexion to match. Athletic looking, he had the slightly bandy legs of the typical Liverpool footballer or boxer and never seemed to stop jogging along even with his full load of Liverpool Echos and Evening Expresses. He carried the newspapers in a canvas bag, "LIVERPOOL ECHO" emblazoned in large red letters on the front, slung over his shoulder. Across the other shoulder, was a leather money-bag on the end of a bandolier and, under his arm, another sheaf of newspapers. As you approached him with a penny, he would slow his pace to a gentle jog, take a paper out of the bag, or from under his arm, fold it once and, like a sleight-of-hand magician, offer it to you with his hand cupped to receive the penny, at the same time, again breaking out into his "Last City Echo, Liverpool Echo" exhortations.

We could still hear Gus two streets away, as he jogged down Lampeter Road, half-way down Townsend Lane.

Chapter 9

I Can't Stop - The Gas Man's Coming

A Waltham Road Red-Letter Day was when the Gas Man paid one of his three-monthly visits to empty the gas meters. He was, without doubt, the most popular of all the callers and the pavements full of children playing hop-scotch, whip-and-top, ollies, ciggies, or whatever, emptied immediately when the Gas Man made his appearance around the corner from the main road.

The Gas Man was always smartly dressed in a semi-uniform of heavy blue serge trousers and a dark blue double-breasted jacket with six polished brass buttons glinting on the front. A Liverpool Gas Company badge was pinned above the fob pocket of the jacket and his peaked cap also carried the words, Liverpool Gas Company. Chained to his right wrist by a short length of brass chain, was a large, black leather Gladstone bag, a shiny brass clasp protecting the cover.

"The Gas Man's coming, Mum", I shouted, as out of breath with excitement, I burst into the kitchen. "He's down the road at the bottom. He's just gone into the Bleasdale's."

"Alright, alright, keep your hair on then, Douglas", said my Mother, "He'll be here shortly."

So saying, she put down her potato-peeler, dried her hands, and, after clearing away the remains of our mid-day meal, threw a blanket over the kitchen table.

The Gas Man didn't have to knock twice.

Escorted by Wally and me, Mother let him in through the front door. He paused at the gas meter behind the vestibule door in the lobby and, with a special key, drew from the innards of the meter a galvanized container full to the brim with copper pennies. He carried it to the kitchen and tipped the pennies in a heap, in the middle of the table.

"Would you like a cup of tea or anything, Mr. Gas Man", my Mother said. He was always called "Mr. Gas Man".

"No thank you, Mrs. Arthur", he replied, "I've just had one at Mrs. Bleasedale's".

Mrs. Bleasedale, earlier that morning, as was her wont, had called at No. 45 to borrow a cupful of sugar from Mum. "I can't stop", she had said. "I've only called to borrow a cup of sugar. And the Gas Man's coming so I can't stop."

Wally and I, watched in awed silence, as the Gas Man lifted his bag onto the table and took out sheets of brown paper. Printed on the shiny side were the words Liverpool Gas Company. Then, with the rapidity of a machine gun he proceeded to count the pennies in piles of thirty (two shillings and sixpence) by sliding them off the table into his hand, stacking the piles in orderly rows on the table. At this point I earned a rebuke from Mother when, in my excitement at spotting my shining, new Christmas Stocking penny in the heap, I nudged the blanket and two of the neat piles of coins toppled over.

"Keep still, Douglas", said Mother, in her quiet but authoritative voice. "Do that again and you'll go upstairs." She knew the Gas Man was in a hurry.

Not at all put out by the collapse of the two columns of coins, the Gas Man carried on counting rapidly, until the heap of pennies was converted into a neat square of coins, like a platoon of infantry standing at attention on parade. Carefully, counting the stacks, firstly from the top to the bottom and then from the bottom to the top, he said to my Mother "One pound ten shillings and three pence, Mrs. Arthur."

Taking an indelible pencil out of his top pocket, he licked the sharp end with his tongue, made a note of the amount in a blue-backed duplicate account book and handed a copy to my Mother. And, to our delight, the Gas Man then handed over to her a handful of the pennies, as he said, "There's your rebate, Mrs. Arthur, one shilling and five pence."

The princely sum of one shilling and five pence was a more-than-welcomed bonus for my Mother, especially during the winter months. And much more welcomed if the Gas Man's visit was on a Thursday, the day before pay-day. Mother reached up and put the coins in the usual place on the mantelpiece reserved for "pennies for the gas". But I knew there would be a penny each for Wally and me after the Gas Man had left and that there would be chips from the chip shop for tea that night and maybe a half of a fish or, a special treat, half of a Which's meat pie.

The Gas Man then proceeded to carry out another conjuring trick with the piles of coins. Placing a stack of thirty pennies on a piece of the printed paper, quick as a flash, he rolled the paper around them, forming a perfect and compact tube lettered on the outside, The Liverpool Gas Company. No glue, or Sellotape or paper clips. Only the paper, neatly folded over to seal the ends of the tube of coins, a perfect example of Liverpool Gas Company origami. Stacking the tubes in his capacious bag and locking it with another key from his key-ring, he clipped the brass chain on to his wrist and was on his way to his next call in Suburban Road.

****

During the endless cold, dark, and fog-blighted winter months, the Boards became a quagmire and reluctantly, we were driven indoors to the empty front room of 45,

Waltham Road, to play ciggies against the wall, and if Father Christmas had been kind at Christmas, and we had been lucky with the stocking, draughts, Ludo and tiddlywinks.

The table game of Shoot, an expensive, but more sophisticated, and more skilful game of tiddlywinks, also was a popular pastime, if any of the gang could raise the money to buy a game.

The Standard game of Shoot was comprised of two teams of opposing tiddlywinks and a white ball. Ten red, and ten blue tiddlywinks, two flickers to dribble the ball, and two tin goalies keeping goal on the goal line of a miniature goal. The more luxurious game of Super Shoot had the same tiddlywinks and flickers but with a more elaborate goal, through which the player could control the goalkeeper by means of a slot in the netting, when his opponent was taking a shot. The price of the Standard game of Shoot was a shilling and the Super game three shillings and sixpence, both well out of range of my meagre pocket money.

It was two or three years later before I was fortunate enough to own a game of Shoot. So to digress again, it is worth recording here, that because of the game of Shoot, I also started my working life at the age of eleven after I had won the game in a National Competition.

Early in 1931, the manufacturers of Shoot held a promotional advertising campaign to flag falling sales. Through newsagents, they issued a flyer advertising the game by the promotion of a competition to complete the blank line of verse on a couplet printed on the back of the leaflet. It seemed easy to me to complete the last line saying something in praise of the game of Shoot. Entries were free and you could enter as many as you wished, providing they were on separate forms. So one afternoon, after school, I called at every newsagent and sweetshop in Anfield and finished up with a dozen or so blank entry forms. I completed each one with a different line and posted them off in one envelope. For my pains I won a shilling game of shoot.

I also got my first job-of-work, for when I called in at Wilson's, the newspaper shop on Townsend Lane, he asked me if I was one of the Arthur boys and offered me a job delivering newspapers.

Chapter 10

The "Cabby"

As soon as we were old enough – four or five, if you were in the charge of an older brother – we were allowed to go to the Cabby. Better known as The Flea-Pit or The Bug-House. In the wintertime, going to the pics on a Saturday afternoon was a must and the Cabbage Hall Picture House, and the dozens of Liverpool cinemas dotted all over the City, were filled every Saturday afternoon, with excited screaming kids.

The Cabbage Hall Picture House was operated and managed by the formidable figure of Mr. Wilkie, with the staunch help of Mrs. Wilkie, the Cashier/Usher/Ice-Cream vendor and vociferous but unsuccessful child-quietener. Mrs. Wilkie issued tickets to the excited patrons from a small opening in a glass fronted circular booth in the tiny foyer at the front entrance to the cinema. In the brief interval, before the big picture started she also sold to those who had the necessary ha'penny or penny, ice-cream and sweets from a large flat tray slung around her shoulders.

Mr. Wilkie did the rest of the work, including, just before the show started, dashing up the back stairs to the projectionist's room to make sure the projectionist knew how to start the film.

An imposing figure of a man in his blue and green uniform and highly polished brown boots, Mr. Wilkie could, himself, have stepped down from the centre of his flickering screen. He wore a large, shiny, blue peaked cap with a white, corded chin-strap across the peak. His green braided, thick, blue-serge jacket sported broad white epaulettes on each shoulder. A greyish/white twisted lanyard coiled out of the top pocket of the jacket and disappeared under the epaulette. His generous stomach, carefully nurtured at the Cabbage Hall Public House, just over the road from the picture house, was held in its rightful place by a wide, green belt with a brass buckle, worn over the jacket.

He was the doorman, marshalling, or attempting to marshal, the two queues of unruly urchins formed up outside before the cinema opened. One queue for the back stalls was at the front entrance of the cinema, under a cracked, unwashed glass canopy, bearing the name CABBAGE HALL PICTURE HOUSE across the front. The other queue for the front stalls, or flea-pit, was down the passage at the side. He collected the tickets as the kids filed in, tearing them in two, handing half back and threading the other half onto a spike attached to a length of cord. The back stalls went in the cinema first and then he dashed down to the bottom side door to let the front stalls in.

At the Cabby Saturday afternoon matinee it was tuppence to luxuriate in the back stalls on a thinly upholstered, tip-up seat, with arm rests. There were no balcony or circle seats. In the front stalls, a penny sat you on a leather-covered, hard seat with your neighbour's elbows jammed in your ribs. However, at the very front of the front stalls, immediately under the dusty, grey screen, a separate section provided three rows of the cheapest of cheap seats for the poorest of the poor patrons. For two clean, undamaged, two-pound glass jam jars from each patron, Mr. Wilkie would forcibly jam nine or ten small children into one of the rough wooden plank seats meant to seat four reasonably sized adults, sometimes having to un-jam them when Little Willie became separated from Lizzie, his six-year-old sister, and set up a howl heard clearly over the pandemonium in the cinema.

A cloth-covered rope hooked across the aisles, half way down the auditorium, was the barrier between the front stalls and the back. Mr. Wilkie, in his spare time in the brief interval, manned the barrier to prevent the patrons of the penny seats upgrading themselves to the tuppenny seats, sometimes to no avail for, inevitably, one or two agile Clarendon Road Bucks, more for devilment than anything else, would drop down to the dirty floor and squirm and wriggle through the discarded chewing-gum, ice-cream cartons and sweet wrappers, until they came to an empty seat in the back stalls. Many years later, they were to be seen doing the same trick, burrowing in the sand under the canvas walls of a tented, Shafto's cinema in a vast Army Camp beneath the Giza Pyramid at Mena, in Egypt, to get in without paying.

The performance started with an ancient black and white Mickey Mouse cartoon, "Steam Boat Mickey", quickly followed by a sing-a-long, accompanied with great gusto by a fat lady at an old, upright piano by the side of the screen. The words of "When-the-Red-Red-Robin-Goes-Bob-Bob-Bobbin-Along" were projected on the screen, a white ball bouncing from word-to-word in time to the thumping of the fat lady on the old piano. Everyone joined in the sing-song, including those who couldn't read!

Just before the brief interval and the start of the big picture, Mr. Wilkie could be seen by those not mesmerized by the black and white antics of Mickey and Minnie Mouse, slowly pacing the three narrow aisles of the little cinema. On his back he carried a large, galvanized container containing a sweet smelling disinfectant or air-freshener. As he walked, his right arm pumped a lever on the side of the container, and a fine spray of disinfectant from a flexible tube held high in his left hand was sprayed over the heads of the spellbound audience, the tiny globules glistening in the searchlight beam of the Mickey Mouse film.

When the ball stopped bouncing, Mr. Wilkie, having

disposed of the tank of smellies, fastened the brass buttons on his jacket, adjusted his shiny peaked cap and donned a pair of white gauntlet gloves, appeared through a curtain behind the piano carrying a six-foot long heavy wooden pole. The noise from the motley crowd of children in the full house, rose to an even higher crescendo. They knew what was coming. Mr. Wilkie stepped towards the centre of the stage, and like Oliver Twist's Workhouse Beagle, heartily thumped the pole, three times, on the wooden floor. There was instant silence for the long awaited big picture.

The eyes of the spellbound audience became glued to the flickering, black and white images on the screen, projected over our heads like a world-war 2 probing searchlight, from a little square of glass high up on the wall opposite, shining through the cloudy haze of rolling dust motes and cigarette smoke. The weekly, scratchy, death-defying episodes of Tom Mix, Buck Jones, and Rin-Tin-Tin kept enthralled the excited audience. The noise alternated between deathly silence and howls of warning as the baddies crept up on Tom, behind his back.

The screeching was only subdued when the never-ending serial of "Edith the Earthwoman" appeared on the screen. In her Spiral Earthworm Machine, Edith could burrow underground, at 30 miles-an-hour to catch the baddies who had just robbed a bank, or she was excavating a road tunnel under a river, just like the Mersey Tunnel being built at that time. Last week's episode had finished abruptly when the River Mersey burst through the roof of the tunnel, the rushing wall of water threatening to flood Liverpool. But, then, to the disappointment and annoyance of the packed house, without warning the hypnotized audience, a large announcement suddenly appeared on the screen.

TO BE CONTINUED NEXT WEEK

Was the Earthworm Machine lost under the River???

DON'T MISS NEXT WEEK'S EPISODE

Next week, Edith rescued the workers before the wall of water reached them, for The Spiral Earthworm Machine turned itself into a submarine, carrying them through the water to the safety of the top of Brownlow Hill, only to be thwarted when a giant sequoia tree in a forest near San Fransisco fell on her underground machine during an earthquake and was

TO BE CONTINUED NEXT WEEK.

I didn't see the next episode so for all I know Edith is still stuck in her Spiral Earthworm Machine under the gigantic fir tree.

By now, Little Willie, jammed tightly between his sister Lizzie and the little Chinese boy from the Chinese Laundry, was completely oblivious of the uproar, and although he had wet his pants with excitement, was fast asleep, snoring gently, his thumb stuck in his mouth.

When the big picture finished, and the baddies had been all safely locked up in jail and Rin-Tin-Tin had successfully rescued the hero off the floating ice-flow, Mr. Wilkie again made his appearance on the stage in front of the screen carrying his thumping pole and wearing his white gauntlets. He pounded the pole three times on the floor to bring to the audience's attention that they should stand for the singing of "God Save The King".

The sepia-tinted picture of the bearded King George V, in his Naval Uniform of an Admiral of the Fleet, appeared on the screen. The fat lady at the piano played the opening bars of the National Anthem and the audience of now somewhat subdued children got on their feet and stood to attention to sing the well known words of the stirring anthem.

Later, when colour had replaced black and white

films on the screens of all cinemas, including the ancient Cabbage Hall Picture House, King George's regal image, a string of large medallions across his chest and wearing the bejewelled Crown of the United Kingdom and a white ermine cape over his shoulders, was superimposed on a brightly coloured, highly detailed picture of a map of the world. Spread across the screen from side to side and top to bottom, the map highlighted in brilliant scarlet, the colonies and territories of the British Empire conquered or colonized by Great Britain, some 25% of the world's population and area. By that time the fat lady had retired and the singing was led by a recording of the anthem played by the massed bands of the regiments of King George's Household Cavalry.

My heart swelled with innocent pride and I started making plans there and then to join the Indian Police or the Canadian Mounted Police or the African Rifles and become a guardian of the British Empire.

I settled for the Territorial Army!

The Cabbage Hall Picture House has long since been the headquarters of Liverpool F. C. Supporters Club.

Chapter 11

The Great Tent And The One-Legged Diver

Once a year, for one week only, the Elders of the Evangelical Gospel Church erected their **GREAT TENT** at Cabbage Hall, on a triangle of wasteland bounded by Lower Breck Road on two sides and Breck Road on the other and facing The Cabbage Hall Picture House. The mobile chapel, throughout the summer preaching the gospel on many different open spaces in Liverpool, once a year had a special service on a Saturday afternoon for the young children of Cabbage Hall. Much to the consternation of Mr. Wilkie, it was very well attended by many of the patrons of his Saturday afternoon matinees.

The Great Tent itself was a great novelty for the children. Especially when it rained. The drumming of the rain on the taut, white canvas almost drowned the chanting of the Lord's Prayer and, until the beginning of the service, there was much giggling and subdued banter, dodging the drips of rainwater falling from unseen holes in the roof. The tent was simply furnished with low wooden forms each side of the central aisle. On a raised platform at one end was a tiny organ alongside a plain wooden table covered by a white cloth. A polished brass Crucifix stood in the middle of the table, the only religious emblem in the Great Tent.

An elderly, white-collared preacher wearing a long, black, skirted frock coat led the short and simple service, starting and ending with the Lord's Prayer; he conducted vigorously the singing of the hymns played on the little organ by another elderly, black-coated person. The organist's thick mop of white hair, mutton chop whiskers and bushy white beard, prompted little Joey Bleasedale, in a moment of silence, to pipe up in his five-year-old falsetto voice, "Is that Jesus there, playing the piano? I didn't know Jesus could play the piano".

There was no sermon and immediately after the opening "Lord's Prayer", for the next thirty minutes or so, the minister led the children into a spirited rendering of the hymns they all knew so well from their scripture lessons at school. "Onward Christian Soldiers" "All Things Bright and Beautiful" "There is a Green Hill far Away".

All were welcome at the hymn singing in The Great Tent and there was no entrance fee or collection. There were "Rednecks", from All Saints Roman Catholic School, "Proddy Dogs" from the Tin School in Townsend Lane and Anfield Road School, my Jewish friend and classmate, Phillip Max, whose mother kept a hat shop in Priory Road, and of course, Stumpy Griffiths, in his bare feet. Stumpy's father was a staunch Orangeman in the Mere Lane Lodge and would have given Stumpy what for if he caught him going in the Great Tent. But, as usual, Stumpy had his own ideas. Even our rivals, the Clarendon Road Bucks attended The Great Tent, sitting in the aisle opposite, doing their best to out-sing the rest of us.

At the end of the lively community singing, the preacher urged us to be sure to go to Sunday School next day, and sent us home clutching illustrated religious tracts to hand to our parents.

****

It always seemed to be raining when Wallis's World Famous Fun Fair made its annual visit to Coney Green at the corner of Priory Road and Utting Avenue, or to the more spacious piece of wasteland behind the Troy Laundry in Cherry Lane. Trudging through the muddy pools around

73

the High Flier, the Bobby Horses, the American Cake-Walk and suchlike rides, I was never certain whether or not it had been worth the effort to save my hard-earned pocket money from the day the placards announcing the coming of the fair had been pasted on the boards at Suburban Road three or four weeks before.

I had managed to save about seven or eight pence, or, if the fair coincided with a visit from the Gas Man, maybe a couple of coppers more. On our first visit on Saturday afternoon, Les Jones and I had spent an hour just walking around in the mud, checking on the price of the rides. They were all well out of the range of our shallow pockets. Thruppence for the High Flyer and the Wall of Death, tuppence for five minutes on the American Cake-Walk or the sedate Bobby Horses. Sixpence was out of the question for the new-fangled Dodgems, and we were too young, anyway, for the Boxing Booth, where if you could last one round with Big Bruiser Bill Bashham, you got your money back and a bonus of a shilling for staying the round.

So we thought we would try our luck on one of the many side stalls offering untold riches for the price of a penny.

My first attempt to acquire a small fortune was on the Roll-A-Penny stall, rolling a penny down a sloping groove onto a draughtboard of black-and-white squares, most of them marked with the symbol 1d. or 2d. To add to the gambling instinct, a few of the squares were glibly marked 1/- or 6d. or 3d, and, really playing on our greed, two larger squares at the back of the board showed an enticing £1.

Seeing our interest, the Roll-A-Penny man fished out of a money-bag slung around his middle a dozen or so pennies and proceeded to roll them casually, down the groove. It was uncanny how he was able to roll five of the pennies onto winning squares as he called, "Easy does it, boys, easy does it. Just try your luck doing it like this". And he would roll another penny, somehow landing it in the middle of the 3d square. I tried my luck. And within seconds had said a sad good-bye to four of my hard-saved pennies. My fist closed over the remaining three pennies in my pocket.

Les said, "Come on Doug leave it and let's try the hoopla stall, or the ball-in-a-bucket. And the dart-board with the playing cards will be a lot easier than that".

The Hoopla-Man was just as eager as the Roll-A-Penny man to get us to try our luck. His stall was decked out with a variety of prizes. Bars of Cadbury's chocolate, alarm clocks, glass vases, china dogs and such like, each standing on a square plywood base. Too late we realized that to win a prize, you had to throw the wooden hoop completely over the prize, and the base, and land it flat on the deck.

"'Ere-yar, lads, two goes for a penny. And you can 'ave a shilling instead of the prize if you win. This is how you do it".

So saying he pulled a wooden hoop, or ring, from the pile threaded on his left arm and with a deft flick of his wrist, threw it, gently, at a two-ounce bar of Cadbury's milk chocolate. The second one he tried landed over the chocolate. "Ther'yare, lads" he said, "It's easy isn't it?" You have a go and I'll give you a bob instead of the chocolate if you get the ring over".

Les's efforts were as bad as mine on the Roll-a-Penny, although he took a few seconds longer to lose his pennies.

So not to be out-done, we tried the Ball-in-the-Bucket - a piece of sleight-of-hand operated as a sideline by the Hoopla-Man

"'Ere," he said. "I'll show you to 'ow to throw the ball in the bucket". "It's as easy as falling off a chair. "

An ordinary galvanized household bucket, tilted towards the thrower at an angle of about 45 degrees, was set back at the side of his stall about three or four feet from a marker. The object was to throw a wooden, cockshy ball from the marker, into the bucket without it bouncing out again and the Hoopla-Man was an expert at this also. He leaned forward, slightly, and with a simple flick of the wrist threw the ball landing it on the side of the bucket, where magically, it whirled round and round before dropping to the bottom with a clatter. "Ther'yare," he said, "A bob, if you can get the ball in the bucket like that. Three goes for a penny. Yer can't lose".

But we did lose. When Les and I threw the balls, they kept bouncing off the bottom of the bucket with a clang, the Hoopla Man catching them on the rebound and keeping the bob in his pocket.

Skint, we decided to kill time and wait for the late afternoon performance of the One-Legged-Diver. The One-Legged-Diver was famous in Liverpool for his daredevil high-dives off the end of New Brighton pier into the muddy waters of the River Mersey. And later made famous throughout the land by Tommy Handley, the first of the great Radio comedians, in his show "ITMA", (It's That Man Again) with his catchphrase, "Don't forget the Diver".

That afternoon The-One-Legged-Diver was going to set himself on fire before making his spectacular, death-defying dive into the six-foot deep, circular water tank. So it was a free show for Les and I, for his diving platform rose twenty or thirty feet high above the tank behind the fenced enclosure and although we wouldn't be able to see him douse himself, we would be able to watch him make his flaming dive off the platform.

So we wandered off, trudging through the mud in the gathering gloom of the cloudy Saturday afternoon, stopping to watch the barkers on the sideshows light their naptha flares. The wicks of these simple flares were black rags stuffed into the end of a long spout of a sooty container, like a watering can, containing the naphtha. Clouds of black smoke stinking strongly of paraffin oil, billowed from the spout, but the flame gave off enough murky illumination for the barkers to see their customers' pennies rolling on to the lines of the squares.

The carousels and merry-go-rounds, with their distinctive oompah-oompah barrel-organ music, were the only attractions on the fairground with electric lights. The multi-coloured bulbs, strung up around the rotating rides and the see-sawing High Flyer, were powered by massive steam engines (steamrollers without the rollers) driving a six-inch wide flapping belt from a gigantic spinning fly-wheel on the side of the engine, to a humming generator situated strategically behind the merry-go-rounds on the edge of the fairground.

We stood mesmerized watching two of the gargantuan monsters in action, their noise drowning the barrel organ thumping of the merry-go-round behind us.

The steam engines were receiving the undivided attention of a tall, painfully thin engineer, who could have been an understudy for Olive Oyl of the Pop-Eye cartoons. Despite the now steady drizzle of rain adding to the pools of mud on the ground, he wore only an oily pair of blue overalls which failed completely to hide his grubby, once white singlet. A damp black cap with a long, shiny peak was perched on the back of his head. In his left hand he held an old piece of rag and in his right a polished, metal oilcan with a long spout. The sweat ran down his face dripping from the end of the drooping cigarette anchored permanently to his lips, as he hopped like a sparrow from engine to engine and generator to generator, putting a dab of oil here, and polishing a brass or copper tube there, seemingly quite unaware of the ear-splitting noise of the machinery. The only time he altered his hop-and-a-skip was when he raked away the red-hot ash collected in the round ash-pan under the roaring fire before stoking it up with fourteen pounds of nutty-slack wielding a huge coal shovel.

Leaving the engineer to his never-ending task of keeping the electric lights burning brightly on both the Merry-Go-Round and the High-Flyer – and it was noticeable how they flickered and dimmed, considerably, if he relaxed his efforts to drink a cup of tea – we made our way back to the booth of the One-Legged-Diver.

We were just in time to see him climbing the ladder to the heady height of the platform on the scaffolding, accompanied by sporadic clapping from the patrons in the enclosure below. He didn't waste time. With one quick movement he bent over to touch his toe, at the same moment springing out and downwards, bringing his arms over his head in line with his one leg, in a perfect high dive. He was enveloped in flames from the waist down and left a trail of red smoke like a comet streaking across the sky and vanished from our view before he reached the tank of water.

The applause this time was loud and prolonged, even from the spectators like Les and I watching from the free side of the enclosure. Before we had time to move, two barkers jostled their noisy way through the crowd, shaking coins in a bucket.

"Don't forget the Diver. Don't forget the Diver".

"Come on Doug", said Les. "I've got tuppence left. But we'll have to forget him this time. Let's go and get some chips from Whiches on the way home".

Chapter 12

"Uncles"

The line of shops each side of Townsend Lane, from the junction of Priory Road at Cabbage Hall, could be likened to today's shopping mall with a limited amount of road traffic; No. 13 and 14 tramcars ploughing their noisy way up and down the single tramline and horse drawn coal carts stopping at the weighbridge on their way to Breck Road Coal sidings.

The weighbridge, or public weighing machine, was a steel plate set in a slip road from Lower Breck Road alongside the weighbridge office, onto which the coal-man manoeuvred his cart into position for weighing. The cart was empty except for a cumbersome, flat steel portable weighing machine, two fourteen pound cast iron weights (many of his customers could only afford to buy fourteen or twenty-eight pounds of coal) and coal sacks folded and stacked neatly to form a comfortable driving seat at the front. The cart, like the black-rimmed eyes of the coal man driving it, still bore evidence of the gritty coal dust from previous loads. The horses, however, were always immaculately groomed, the leather harnesses, and horse brasses, polished and shining as if they were going on to the May Day Parade. After loading the coal at the depot, on his return the coal man would weigh the loaded cart again on the weighbridge.

Burdened with double-tiered loads of forty 1cwt. bags of coal many of the carts were hauled by teams of four huge shire horses, a magnificent sight, particularly on cold winter days, as they puffed and snorted their way up the incline of Townsend Lane with flared nostrils blowing clouds of steam and sparks flying from their steel-shod hooves clipping the granite sets of the road.

A sandstone horse trough was set on the pavement edge of Breck Road just beyond the weighbridge, alongside an ornate, marble, public drinking fountain complete with a metal drinking cup on the end of a chain attached to the fountain. So Cabbage Hall became a sort of pit-stop for the horses to take a breather after the long haul up the incline of Townsend Lane before tackling the somewhat steeper hill of Breck Road.

****

Next door to the weighbridge office was the "Herb Shop".

The Herb Shop was a favourite meeting place for the kids of Waltham Road if they had a ha'penny to spare. A cross between a chemists shop and an ice-cream parlour, the Herby's mysterious atmosphere was laden with aromatic herbal scents and smells. To add to the mystery, the herbalist, gliding silently like a black ghost from behind a heavy curtain at the back, miraculously always made an appearance as soon as you entered the shop. She was a lanky, thin, elderly woman dressed in a dark, flowing skirt reaching to her feet. Her once jet-black hair was streaked with grey, which though coiled up in the form of a knot, failed to conceal three greyish-white carbuncles the size of golf balls, nestled like hen's eggs on the top of her head. She was an object of much whispered discussion by the kids as, sitting at the little table under the window, they sipped their hot Sarsaparilla and Soda water drinks. Whispered, because the "Black Witch" - as the kids had christened her - did not allow hilarity or robust conversation. A sharp word of rebuke from her led to a hasty supping of the hot drinks and a quick exit from the shop.

A long, high counter stretched from wall to wall of the shop, with at one end a large, clear glass jar labelled across the front FANTAS SODA, a bubble of air in the clear water making its way from the bottom to the top of the jar every minute or so. Behind the counter the wall was lined with shelves holding brown, salt-glazed earthenware containers each with a miniature, polished brass draw-off tap at the bottom and a conical shaped lid topped with a round, brass knob. Etched in black Old-English characters, they all bore the name of a herb. Rosemary, Saffron, Sarsaparilla, Liquorice, Ginger, Dandelion-and-burdock. Underneath the shelves was a series of tiny drawers each neatly labelled with a white card fitting into a brass clip. But the crowning glory of the Herby was on the top shelf. Four huge red, blue, green and yellow empty glass jars, or jeroboams, with fluted sides and long narrow necks. Three flickering gas wall lights on the wall behind them bathed the shop in a soft, colourful glow and added to the mysterious attraction of the Townsend Lane Herb Shop.

Galloways the pawnbrokers, or "Uncles" as it was more popularly known, on the corner of Waltham Road and Townsend Lane, was the biggest, the busiest, and the most prosperous establishment in Cabbage Hall. On fine days Uncles' sign over the shabby emporium could be seen from the top of Breck Road; the familiar and ancient sign of the pawnbroker; three brass balls as big as footballs hanging, pyramid shaped, in an iron framework on the wall over the entrance to the shop.

Uncles had two windows, the main one facing Townsend Lane and the other around the corner in Waltham Road. The larger window, protected by a thin wire mesh on the inside and a heavier metal grill on the outside, was an Aladdin's Cave of gold and silver, pearl necklaces, diamond rings, watches, clocks, snuff-boxes, hair-brushes, a tray full of war medals with their coloured ribbons, and hanging from the wall at the back, a somewhat moth-eaten fox-fur ladies stole, its glass eyes reflecting the bright light from the recently installed electric bulbs surrounding the inside of the window frame. The pawnbroker's window was a veritable treasure-trove, gleaned for the most part from the out-of-work residents and ex-soldiers of the terraced houses of Townsend Lane and Breck Road.

In one corner of the window, however, hung a display of Ingersoll pocket watches and chains dangling from a card showing the price - 1s/11d - in large figures, which had become an insignificant, but well remembered milestone in my life. I had proudly received one of these valuable watches from my Mother for my 5th Birthday, as did all my other brothers on their 5th birthdays, together with a copy of the Holy Bible from Granny Sheel.

The somewhat smaller window in Waltham Road, around the corner, was crammed willy-nilly, from top to bottom, with an assortment of cotton bed sheets, fluffy grey and red blankets, white damask tablecloths, brown lace-up boots and highly polished black shoes. And hanging from the back, two blue-serge gents three-piece suits alongside a banjo in its open frayed case, a mandolin with most of the strings missing, a brass trombone in need of a good polishing and a tall, black top hat with black ribbons around the brim. Unredeemed pledges.

Fortunately, I wasn't a regular customer, although I have to say that Father's Sunday-Best-Blue-Serge-Suit occasionally went in hock at Uncles, usually in an emergency on a Thursday afternoon when Father was skint and had run out of cigarettes. He couldn't live without his cigarettes and made Mother's life a misery if he hadn't got any. And everybody else had to keep out of his way, too. So sometimes, Mother had to take his suit in to Uncles on a Thursday to get his cigarette money and I redeemed it after Father came home with his wages on a Friday night. In the winter months I would wait until after dark, so I could sneak in without anybody seeing me.

There was also one well-remembered occasion, when the Gas Man was due but hadn't turned up, and Mother didn't even have the money to buy a threepeny ham shank for tea. So with time on her hands she "borrowed" Father's silver hunter pocket watch and chain, telling him that she had taken it to the watch repairer to have it cleaned and serviced. Father thought the service charge was too high!

I hated the pawnshop.

I hated the dark, gloomy entrance of the Pledge Office at the side of the shop in Waltham Road, with its musty, stale smell tinged with the scent of mothballs and camphor. And I hated the storeroom behind the high counter, packed from floor to ceiling with what appeared to be the contents of everybody's wardrobe or airing cupboard. Most of all I hated the condescending, baldy-headed assistant, with the permanent runny nose and the dirty-looking grey warehouseman's overall, who always gave me the impression he was doing me a favour when he handed back to me Father's Sunday-Best-Blue-Serge-Suit.

Chapter 13

Which Is Next?

On the other hand, I loved Metcalf's the fish-and-chip shop on the corner of Waltham Road opposite Uncles. I loved the sound of the sizzling fish-and–chips and I loved the warm, comforting, homely smell of the shop, unsullied by the spicy aroma of Indian curry and Oriental sweet and sour. I loved the warm welcoming smile of the white coated, motherly Mrs. Metcalf, who when finishing serving one customer, would look up at the queue, saying, with a smile, "Which is next, which is next?" Metcalf's the chippy, christened forever by the Arthur Family, "Which's the Chippy".

Most of all, I loved Which's hot, savoury, pork pies. Crusty, dark brown oval pies filled with tender pork-meat swimming in a bath of dark onion gravy. Regretfully, a whole pie to myself was too expensive and had to be shared with Wally and it was many years before I had the luxury of eating a whole Which's pie for myself. Their pork pies were a speciality of the house, in my opinion far outclassing the cold tripe and trotters laid out on trays in the window and even the thick breaded fish cakes made on the premises by Mrs. Metcalf.

Fish-and-chips, battered potato scallops and fingers, pork pies and tripe-and-trotters, were dispensed with green mushy peas by Mrs. Metcalf from behind a high wooden counter, its top scrubbed a gleaming white. In the middle of the counter stood two white enamelled saltcellars and a vinegar dispenser, alongside a neat pile of newspapers and smaller squares of grease proof paper. With sleight-of-hand worthy of a magician at the Liverpool Empire, she could sprinkle salt and vinegar on to a portion of chips and wrap them up in the newspaper in a twinkling of an eye. Alongside the paper stood a galvanized cash till, its figures when she rung up the sale, appearing just above the counter level with my nose. Red for silver, black for copper. Nailed into the counter top, just in front of the cash till, was a two-shilling piece. "It was made out of lead", Mother said, in response to my query. "Nailed there as a warning not to try passing counterfeit coins."

I was fascinated by the culinary activity behind the counter and although my mouth was watering in anticipation and my stomach rumbling loudly with the permanent hunger of a nine-year-old, I would sometimes lose my place in the queue to watch Mr. Metcalf. He was the cook, the potato chipper and the dipper of the fillets of cod into a bowl of thick batter before expertly dropping them into the boiling fat. He stoked the two square coal fires under the vats of bubbling fat, and with a wire scoop, would swirl the chips about in the fat and then, with bare fingers, pick one out to see if they were cooked. "Never try that at home, sonny", he said to me on one occasion, "I've got asbestos fingers".

He also chipped the potatoes with a long, lever-handled potato-chipper fixed at the end of the counter. I would stand in front of him watching carefully as, with a quick, rhythmical movement, in five minutes he turned a bucket of peeled potatoes into chips. Taking a potato from the bucket alongside the chipper, he would balance it on the squares under the handle of the machine and in one lightning movement move his left hand away from the potato as he brought his right arm down with a thump, shaking the counter, to produce a dozen symmetrical chips. Wide eyed I waited in vain to see him chip off the ends of his fingers, wondering if he would put the bits in the fryer with the chips.

I was determined to have a fish-and-chip shop as soon as I grew up.

++++++++++++++++

You could buy almost anything in the Townsend Lane parade of shops. You didn't need to worry about going into town to Newshams, the Credit Drapers, for a new suit if all you could afford was a second-hand one from Uncles and you weren't too much worried that you thought it may have once belonged to Norman Smith from Clarendon Road.

The large square brass plate by the open door of the Cabbage Hall Surgery, proclaiming Dr. Bogle's medical qualifications, was polished every day. The Surgery was open afternoon and evenings. You didn't need to make an appointment and if you had his 2/6 fee you would get in to see him within five or ten minutes and almost certain go home with a bottle of what looked like coloured water. Although I don't ever remember me, or my brothers ever having to go and see him, and Dad, who needed the doctor more than any of us, treated himself with Liquid Paraffin or McCleans Stomach Powder

Purslow's the pork butcher and "Purveyor of Quality Meats", took pride of place in the middle of the block. Fresh sawdust was strewn every day on the floor of the butchers, and in wet weather the shop was unmistakable, for a damp trail of wood shavings left its mark from the door, disappearing from view on the pavement in Townsend Lane.

Mr Purslow was renowned in Cabbage Hall for his free soup. In the icy cold of the depths of mid-winter, when the ground had almost turned into Siberian permafrost, Mr. Purslow brewed the soup from left over bones and gristle and fatty waste, in an old army field kitchen in his backyard. When the word got around that smoke was billowing over the top of the wall in the back entry, accompanied by a distinctive pong, you knew he was making his soup. I joined the queue once with Stumpy Griffiths, (still in his bare feet) and proudly carried home a jugful of the stuff, but Mum never used it because, she said, she didn't fancy the smell or the fat floating in glistening globules on the top. Strangely, many years later, I was reminded of this soup, amidst bouts of wishful thinking and homesickness, when I was ladled a cup of watery horse-soup, with the compliments of Herr Hitler, in a concentration camp en route to Germany.

The Abbey Road Bakery, opposite, always attracted an audience of kids when Ranks flour wagon made a delivery. They stood and watched the sacks of flour being unloaded and hauled up to the top floor by hydraulic hoist. And for a small charge, Mother, and Mrs. Bleasdale, before gas cookers had found their way to Waltham Road, would take spiced bun-loaves and risen dough to be baked in the bread ovens after the night-time bread baking was finished.

Next door was Harrisons, the "Gentlemen's Outfitters", where my older brothers could get all the "necessities for the well-dressed man-about-town", from collar studs to cuff links and bowler hats to brown boots. Periodically, I would go to Harrisons to buy those stiff white collars for my Father which I took every week to the Chinese Laundry's Opium Den. There was a printed notice on the wall behind the counter at Harrisons, which the eye couldn't fail to see.

PLEASE DO NOT ASK FOR CREDIT
AS A REFUSAL OFTEN OFFENDS

And of course there was an Irwins.

"IRWINS THE GROCERS" shops, one of the forerunners of the great Tesco Empire, were unmistakable and could be found in almost every main shopping street on Merseyside. Their shop-fronts, glazed with shiny, maroon and gold tiles with the name IRWINS highlighted in gold letters over the door, stood out from the other shops in the block. At Cabbage Hall, there was an Irwins in Townsend Lane and two more a short way up the road in Breck Road.

Irwins shop was a favourite of mine. The assistants were always friendly and helpful, even to a ten year old shopping for his mother, no doubt being fully aware that she was the mother of a growing family of five boys and two girls. Later, I did the grocery shopping there, in my lunch hour, for Miss Wilson, the owner of the newsagents and tobacconists, when I worked there delivering newspapers.

The shop, except for the sawdust-strewn customer area in the centre, was packed from floor to ceiling with glamorous groceries and fancy foodstuffs of all kinds from all over the world. Fixed to the ceiling around three sides of the shop was a polished steel rail, from which hung, on "S" hooks, long cloth covered "sides" of bacon, plump smoked hams, round yellow, red and white cheeses and at Christmas time, feathered turkeys and ducks and chickens, their heads dangling down just above my head. On my request for "Half-a-pound of smoked rhoded bacon, please" the white-coated assistant had no hesitation in using the long pole with the hook on the end, to take down from the ceiling-rail a side of bacon weighing half a hundredweight, place it on the hand-operated bacon slicer, cut off three or four slices and then hoisting it back up again to the ceiling.

At one end of the counter was the "Butter Basher", a young apprentice practising the grocer's gentle art of "Butter Bashing". Armed with two flat, wooden paddles, he stood in front of a block of buttercup yellow butter on a white marble slab. After dipping his paddles in a bowl of cold water, he would use them to take off a portion of butter from the block, weigh it exactly to a half pound and deftly "bash" it into a neat oblong before reversing his paddle to leave an imprint of a country scene on one side of the butter and then wrapping it in a grease-proof paper labelled, "Irwins Best Danish Keil Butter". Miss Wilson always insisted on Danish Keil butter and no other was acceptable. Unfortunately, it was a little too expensive for my Mother's purse and we had to make do with best Irish margarine.

At the other end of the counter, Charlie Hawkins, another young trainee, was seated alongside a straw-filled tea chest. He was patiently picking out eggs from the straw-filled tea chest, which, he told me later, had just completed their long and tedious sea journey from Peking in China. Holding an egg up to the electric lamp in front of him, evidently he could tell if the egg had turned bad. The good ones he placed in a square, shaped egg-tray and the bad ones he threw into a bucket. The trays of eggs in the window bore the sign, **Fresh eggs. ½d each. Six for 2 ½d**.

Then there was Ashtons the Greengrocers, the owners of the frightening piebald pony. Mrs Ashton always complimented me when, doing the weekly shop for my Mother, I would reel off a list of ten or twelve items from memory. "You'll be Prime Minister one day" said Mrs. Ashton, "If you keep that up". I didn't tell her that my Mother could recite, from memory, all the books of the Holy Bible, from beginning to end, and then as an encore recite them all again, from the end to the beginning. And she never got to be Prime Minister! And invariably, Mrs. Ashton would say "Are you sure you'll be able to manage to carry all that lot back home. Here, I'll lend you this box. Make sure you let me have it back".

Next door to Ashtons, was Audsleys the cake and sweet shop, where you could get the best "Wet Nellies", the biggest gob-stoppers and the thickest "sticky-lice" liquorice root in Liverpool . And they did a roaring trade with their speciality – round sugared jam doughnuts, two for threeha'pence – made on the premises.

Long before Do-it-Yourself was ever thought of, Storah's The Chandler, stocked everything for the family which had to do its own house repairs and maintenance. Gas mantles, paraffin oil, blowlamps and blowlamp prickers, gloss paint, distemper and whitewash, 2" x 2" timber and 4" floorboards. The list was endless and if you wanted a Belfast sink, or one of those new-fangled electric hair-dryers, and he didn't have it in stock, he would get it for you the next day. And for the hard-up mothers of Townsend Lane who had run out of coal on a windy sub-zero Thursday, and hadn't the money for a bag of coal, he stocked cheap "brickets" and "eggs" made out of coal dust, to put them over until Friday pay day. Mr. Storah, calloused hands ingrained with the dirt and grease of years of delving into bags of six inch nails and cutting rolls of perforated zinc into twelve inch squares for back-kitchen meat safes, was ever present in his shop except for Sundays. He was a fountain of knowledge about all things in the hardware and building repair business.

"What can I get you", he would say.

"A pair of six inch japanned hinges for a door, " came the reply.

"What sort of door?"

"It's for our back door, the old ones have rusted away"

"Well you want a pair of fifteen inch, then", he would say.

****

And, a short walk up the road was the Rawdon Public Library and Reading Room, one of the oldest libraries in Liverpool. On my seventh birthday Mother took me up to the Rawdon. I scribbled my name on a form and she signed the back of it and I was a member. I could borrow a book of my choice and keep it for fourteen days and it didn't cost me a penny. I couldn't believe my luck and was a regular borrower at the Rawdon Library until I went in the Army twelve years later.

For most of those years, I was in awe of the Rawdon, obeying their Rules without question. And their Golden Rule was **SILENCE**. Gently, but firmly enforced with sibilant shushing and hissing and raising of the eyebrows by the lady librarians on the other side of the high counter, and the unspoken threat of having your free ticket taken away.

The Rawdon was split into two sections. The library, its shelves stacked with plain, hard-backed books, facing you as you came through the massive glass panelled double doors, and the Reading Room the other side of another pair of swing doors. **SILENCE** was engraved, prominently in black letters on the glass, and in case you didn't see it, again over the top of the doors. The Reading Room was strictly for adults, and standing on tip-toe I could just see through the glass door old men in flat, cloth caps and white silk scarves around their necks, picking out the winners (and the losers) in the Daily Herald or News Chronicle and the Racing News, spread out on the tables. In wintertime they were all crowded around the tables nearest the huge cast iron fluted radiators.

The Junior Department was the end section of the Adult Library. There were no Tiger-Tim annuals, coloured, monthly magazines or paperback books. The hard backed books, the names of the authors in alphabetical order on the shelves, displayed only the title and name of the author on the spine and you made a selection by pushing the book through to the other side of the shelf. If I wanted a book from the top shelf, by Adams or Alcott or Blake or Billy-the- Kid, I had to ask an adult to push it through for me. It was strictly against the rules to pull the book off the shelf to peruse the contents. One of the librarians at the rear of the shelves then collected it, called out the name of the book, took your card and placed it with the slip from the book into a file where it was kept for fourteen days. If you hadn't got your card then you didn't get the book.

Over the years at the Rawdon, I progressed from The Wind in the Willows and Pooh Bear to Treasure Island, Tom Sawyer, Teddy Lester's Schooldays, A Tale of Two Cities, The Man In The Iron Mask and then, reading mainly on the tram going to and from work, P.C. Wren, Rafael Sabbatini, G.K.Chesterton, Edgar Wallace and Agatha Christie.

Chapter 14

A Sunday Walk To Stanley Park

Waltham Road was well placed for access to the few green open spaces of smoke-begrimed Liverpool of yesteryear. On the doorstep of Breck Park, itself an extensive recreation ground with tennis courts and bowling greens, and baseball and football pitches, Waltham Road was also within easy walking distance of two of Liverpool's most beautiful landscaped parks, Newsham and Stanley.

One warm, sunny Sunday morning, mother said to me "Doug. It's a lovely day today, what about taking the girls for a walk to Newsham Park? Or, I tell you what, go to Stanley Park. You'll just be in time to see the cuckoo on the floral clock. It'll be popping out at ten o'clock and the flowers are in full bloom now. The girls would love to see it. You should be there, easily, by ten. And on the way home, you can call at your Auntie May's. But don't forget. Be back in time for Sunday School. "

I thought a walk to Stanley Park, followed by a visit to the Arthur's in nearby Ince Avenue, was a good idea. There was always a Sunday penny from Uncle Harry "to buy ice-cream on the way home" when we visited Aunty May and Uncle Harry. And if my eldest cousin, Lenny, was out of bed there was sometimes another penny for a bottle of Dandelion-and-Burdock from the herb shop in Townsend Lane, in the afternoon. And I couldn't see how I could get back in time for Sunday School.

Sunday mornings at 45 Waltham Road was bath-time and hair-washing time and time for the family's weekly change of clothes into Sunday Best, all of which had to last until the following Sunday.

The oval, galvanized tin bath, hanging from a six-inch nail on the back-yard wall opposite the kitchen door, had been taken down and placed in front of the fire in the grate. The black iron kettle on the hob, together with two extra saucepans squeezed onto the fire, barely provided enough hot water to cover the bottom of the tin bath. But, just the same, two-at-a-time, in lukewarm water barely covering our legs, and after the usual argument about who should sit at the sloping end of the bath, nearest the fire, we had received our weekly scrubbing from Mum flavoured with her breathless comments that "thank goodness the Nit Nurse in school, last week, had said there were no nits in your hair, I've heard that half the kids in Anfield Road School were alive with them, and we could do with a haircut anyway, and when did you get that scratch, and hurry up and get dried or you'll catch your death of cold."

After the scrub in the bath I had plastered down my unruly hair with Corporation Hair-Oil from the cold-water tap in the back kitchen, and despite the rapidly rising temperature of an August heat wave, I was rigged out in the standard winter (or summer) garb-of-the-day for eight year olds.

My 'combs'- a thick, one-piece, combination singlet-and-underpants woollen garment worn next to my skinny frame - was already making itself felt in the prickly heat, under a clean white open-necked "cricket" shirt. Over the shirt was a heavy, red and blue striped, woollen jersey with a floppy collar. The combs and shirt and jersey were tucked inside worsted, blue-serge short trousers, or pants, hand-me-downs from older brother Ken, originally made by mother from a discarded suit of father's. Holding up the pants under my jersey, were two-inch wide, red-and-blue braces, the leather eyelets of which were threaded through holes in the jersey and fastened to buttons on the pants thus providing ease of access when visiting the lavatory at the bottom of the yard. Those fancy attachments earned me the nickname "Braces" which stuck with me until I started school when I became "Tich". My boots, though down-at-heel and cracked across the toecap, had been cleaned and polished by mother. Darned grey, woollen socks, covering my legs from ankle to knee, completed my summer (and winter) attire. They were held in place by a short length of black elastic, the ends sown together with cotton, to form a garter. By the time we got back home, I would have pulled down the thick socks over my ankles and the rumpled jersey would be tied around my waist by the sleeves.

Setting out with Rene and Jean, holding on to the girls' hands, I crossed over Townsend Lane and turned in to Priory Road heading for the Park. Traffic was almost non-existent. Private cars in those days were few and far between and even the clip-clop, clip-clop of horses pulling coal carts and milk floats and bread carts was strangely silent. Horses also had to have their day of rest. The bone-shaker trams did not run along Priory Road and the shops were closed. So Priory Road almost had the peaceful serenity of a country lane as we walked along the broad pavement, passing under the welcome shade of bulbous, knotty plane trees growing in squares of bull-nosed kerbstones every fifty yards or so. Sunday morning church bells were ringing. The rolling chimes of St. Simon and St. Jude's in Anfield Road in competition with those of Holy Trinity in Breck Road and All Saints in Oakfields.

We got as far as Douglas Road when one of the kids asked if we could go and see the "moo-cows" in the Dairy on the way, so we left Priory Road and turned up Douglas Road. At the top, we saw Mr. and Mrs. Seth Jones, our neighbours from No. 43 next door, also dressed in their Sunday best, going into the Welsh Presbyterian Church. The Welsh church – one of the few Welsh churches in

Liverpool - was opposite the Boys Department of Anfield Road Council School, where, earlier that year, I had joined the Junior Boys.

The school playing ground was strangely empty except for Jackie Jones and his brother, Monty, from Winchester Road. They had climbed over the railings to play cricket with their new homemade bat made that morning from an old piece of floorboard. With a threadbare tennis ball, they were playing against one of the wickets painted on the walls of the school. Jackie called me to climb over and join them for an over or two. I was tempted for a minute or so but my mind was suddenly made up for me when the Jones brothers made a hurried exit over the wall in the Boys' Lavatory next to the Woodwork Centre, when the Caretaker, Mr. Wilkinson, came out of the door of the Junior School. The school was out of bounds at the weekends, and anyway playing games on a Sunday was strictly out of order.

Regretting the lost game of cricket we crossed over the junction of Anfield Road and Walton Breck Road, passing Gallachers' sweet-shop – closed for the day - at the corner of Douglas Road. Jean, my future sister-in-law, worked at Gallachers'. On the opposite corner was Walker's flatiron pub, a well-known watering hole for both Liverpool and Everton supporters on the way to a Home game on a Saturday afternoon. The cows and the dairy were just a short walk from the corner.

Sayers' dairy was one of the few shops open on Sundays. Fresh milk, eggs, butter and cream could be bought until mid-day. The spotlessly clean shop was empty except for a carefully formed pyramid of brown, speckled eggs, balanced, precariously, in a large, round wicker basket at one end of the mottled marble-topped counter. Alongside the basket was an ornate, red and brown glazed piece of pottery in the shape of a hen with beady black eyes and a brilliant red coxcomb, roosting on a nest in the middle of the round bowl. A sign in front of the basket of eggs, written on a page of a lined exercise book in heavy blue copperplate said, **New Laid Eggs. 1d each. 7 for 6d.** I wondered "who would be able to afford to buy six eggs at one time?" Two polished galvanized milk churns stood on the floor at the other end of the counter and three spiky, faded-green anaemic looking plants were overflowing from huge green-glazed bulbous flowerpots standing on the floor under the window. The clean, shiny, white-tiled walls of the shop were hung with brightly coloured posters depicting massive, healthy-looking brown cattle with long ferocious horns curling out of their heads, standing up to their knees in lush, green grass and clumps of yellow buttercups and dandelions. In the centre of the wall, behind the counter, was another country landscape, a pastoral picture in glazed tiles recessed into the white tiles. A matching dado of brightly coloured tiles ran around the walls.

Mr. Sayers had already delivered milk to our house earlier that morning in his chariot-like milk float.

His smart pony-and-trap, the glossy, brown and black varnished woodwork of the carriage, and the polished brass harness fittings of the horse glistening in the morning sun, rode grandly on two iron-shod, wooden wheels taller than me. Carved spokes radiated from a grease-laden hub in the centre. Like most milk floats, before tramcars had made their appearance, it doubled up as a hansom cab taxiing passengers down to Lime Street station. Mr Sayers had been on the corner of Waltham Road and Suburban Road, with his milk, at about half past eight that morning, and I had collected our usual two pints from him. The cows had been milked first thing and the still warm milk was carried in four galvanized milk churns standing in the deep well of the carriage between the two passenger seats each side. Old Sayers stood on the sunken step at the rear of the carriage, like a Roman Charioteer in his chariot, holding two leather reins stretching over the churns and across the cart to the mouth of Bluey the black-and-white pony harnessed between the long wooden shafts. A thin, flexible whip, standing upright in its scabbard on the side of the chariot, completed the picture of the Roman Charioteer.

At twopence-ha'penny a pint, the milkman dispensed the milk, a pint or a gill at a time, from a galvanized scoop, carried hooked over the inside of the churn. Mother had said, "Doug, go and get two pints. And make sure he fills the measure before he empties it into your jug." But Mr. Sayers, his long arm dipping into the depths of the churn, was always too quick for me. I was never quite sure whether he had spilt any out of the measure, back into the churn, on its quick transfer to my jug.

Now, however, the milk float was standing empty outside the dairy yard, its two long shafts pointing at an angle to the sky, like the masts of the yachts on Meols beach waiting for the tide to come in. The pony stood in the end stall of a cowshed on the other side of the yard contentedly munching his way through a trough of hay. Four black and white cows were also tethered in the shed their rears facing us as we stood in a line at the gate of the yard. Their dirt-encrusted tails swished, ceaselessly, from side to side, disturbing clouds of buzzing bluebottles and flies, to send them circling over their rumps to alight again when the tails stopped their swishing. Not a bit like the cows in the country scenes of the posters on the wall of the dairy.

"Ugh", said Jean, holding my hand tightly, "It doesn't half smell."

"Never mind that", I replied, "But that's where your milk comes from."

"Well", she said, "I'm never going to ever drink milk again. "

In one corner of the cobbled yard stood a wooden henhouse, obviously in need of some repair, for the felt on the roof was peeling off exposing cracked and broken woodwork. Two hens, apparently fast asleep, roosted on a long gangplank arrangement from the little door of the coop to the muddy floor. In the other corner of the yard stood a huge mountain of steaming manure, a gooey, brown sludge leaking from the base to form a thick rivulet oozing its way to a grid in the centre of the yard. Mr. Sayers, surrounded by a dozen or so brown hens, noisily scrabbling around in the mud at his feet, was forking manure from a battered rusty wheelbarrow, adding to the mountain of muck.

Mr. Sayers, the Dairyman/farmer, was not my idea at all of what a farmer should look like. Mind you, to be honest, I had never seen a farmer in my life, except for coloured illustrations in my sisters' "Book of English Nursery Rhymes". These depicted a red-faced, perspiring jovial countryman, with an extra large stomach spilling over a huge brass buckle in the centre of a wide black belt. He wore a bright red bandana around his neck and a large straw hat perched precariously on the back of his head, He was mopping the sweat off his sunburnt brow with a black-and-white handkerchief because, apparently, He Had Lost His Wife. And, Old Macdonald Who Had A Farm was certainly nothing like him.

Mr. Sayers was tall and scraggy with a thick, grey drooping moustache, and a permanent, mournful expression on his face. Even when he was serving milk from the churn, the stump of a cigarette always dangled from the corner of his mouth. He had changed his off-white dairyman's coat from his early morning milk deliveries and had donned a faded, one-piece, blue bib-and-brace overall, the braces of which kept continually slipping off one shoulder to expose a grubby white vest. His dungarees were hitched up with a piece of string tied around his legs below his knees to keep the ends from dragging in the muck. Without much success, really, for the frayed trouser legs dripped brown slurry.

He was emptying the contents of the wheelbarrow on to the steaming midden with a large flat shovel, accompanying each dripping shovelful with a distinctive grunt or groan as he threw it to the top of the heap, like a heavyweight boxer in the tenth round of an energy-sapping contest throwing a weary punch at his opponent.

As he finished, he turned around and spotted us at the gate. Throwing his fag-end on the dung-heap, he grunted again, noisily cleared his throat, spat into the pile and said "Worra you lot doin, 'angin' around 'ere for? Clear off."

It wasn't very long after this Sunday Outing that Sayers Dairy and similar back street cow-keepers closed down when the Liverpool Wholesale Co-operative Society opened its first cow-less dairy in Priory Road and delivered bottled milk at half-past six in the morning.

Not in the least crestfallen - the girls had had their fill of moo-cows anyway - carrying on down Arkles Road, we crossed over Anfield Road and made our way down Arkles Lane to the Park entrance. In Arkles Lane, street sweepers were cleaning up the rubbish and litter and cigarette ends left by the 20,000 odd crowd at Liverpool's friendly, pre-season Derby game, against Everton, the day before. We had to wait to cross over the wide double road until the rickety No. 43A tram from the Pier Head had made its deafening, swaying passage across the junction, on its noisy journey down the central tram-track to Carr Lane and Norris Green, via the Troy Laundry at Cherry Lane.

A Wall's Stop-Me-And-Buy-One ice-cream tricycle was parked invitingly on the corner near the park gates, its dark blue and white livery standing out against the green of the trees. Mr. Wall, dressed in a matching blue and white jacket and a large flat-topped, Soviet Field-Marshall's style cap, with a Walls' "Stop-Me-And-Buy-One" sign above the shiny peak, sat on the saddle of the trike smoking a cigarette. From time to time ringing a large round bell on the handlebars and, although he was stationary, calling "Stop me and buy one, stop me and buy one" to the audience of the younger end of the Arthur Family.

He was out of luck. And so was I. And so was Jean, who as soon as she saw the Lollypop Man had let go of my hand and ran towards him, wailing, "Can we have a lolly, Doug, can we have a lolly". The Lollypop Man had already leaned over in anticipation of an early Sunday morning sale taking off the heavy lid on the top of his icebox, as Jean got to him. But my trouser pockets were empty except for a large hole in one, and in the other, a dirty hanky from last week which I had forgotten to put in the wash. I had to drag the protesting Jean away from the tricycle, my parched mouth also watering at the thought of Mr. Wall delving into the well-known contents of the icebox for one his Snofruits, the triangular-shaped, strawberry-flavoured, iced lollies. The Snofruits, at a penny each - just about in our price range if we had been to Uncle Harry's - were the least expensive delicacies in his mobile refrigerator. The ice cream proper ranged from twopence for a vanilla brickette, to one-and-sixpence for a large, family-size raspberry whirl. It went through my mind that it might possibly have been a better idea if we had gone to Uncle Harry's first.

We paused at the open, majestic wrought iron gates of Stanley Park - as I usually did every time I went to the park - to read the notice fixed to the railings alongside the gates. Old English letters picked out in gold leaf, prominent against the black painted board, proclaimed, amongst other legal jargon I didn't understand, that it was an offence to drop litter or chewing-gum in the park, and to spit; and that dogs must be kept on a lead, and, under the penalty of a heavy fine, it was forbidden to pick the flowers. And, highlighted,

Please Keep Off The Grass

And, most importantly, and somehow threateningly, in larger gold leaf letters across the top,

**THIS PARK WILL CLOSE ONE HOUR
AFTER SUNSET AND THE
GATES WILL BE LOCKED**

Making a mental note that I would have to be careful not to be locked in the park with the kids, after dark, we strolled on along the neat, gravelled path which ran the length of the park alongside the playing field and the boating lake, Jean still going on about being thirsty and wanting an iced-lolly.

The path, meandering through the park, was fenced in, each side, by an eighteen inch high, green painted, round-topped, iron railing. The ornamental rails, with neat, clipped, grass verges on the other side of them, separated the path from high, overgrown rhododendron bushes. The thicket of bushes on one side bordered Stanley Park Playing Field, where later, I was to play football and baseball for Anfield Road Elementary School. On the other side, the bushes hid the boundary railings of the park, which, later still, together with the imposing iron entrance gates of the park, were to be melted down and dropped on Berlin. At intervals, small cast iron plaques were set into the grass verges, some of them flat on the grass and some standing upright in the turf, on spikes. The neatly painted letters cast into the surface of the plaques, bore the important, but polite message.

PLEASE KEEP OFF THE GRASS

These plaques also, were destined to end up as pieces of shrapnel in a Berlin park, together with the railings from the paths.

It looked as if someone had ignored the request however, when, shortly, we bumped into a park keeper – the"Parkie" . He was lugging along by the lobes of their ears, two boys of about my own age. One of them was in his bare feet and, as they said in Liverpool those days, "the arse of his kecks was battering his brains out". I was sorry for the untidy, unkempt, unwashed lads and wondered what they had been up to. As they passed, I heard the Parkie saying, "I've told you before, you little buggers, don't run all over the flower beds. Gerroff home if you've got one and don't let me see you 'ere agen."

Every few yards, park benches were recessed into the edge of the path, under the shade of the high bushes, each with a wire litter basket and a bed of flowers alongside. The low ornamental railings were diverted around the benches which were mostly occupied by elderly gentlemen with peaked caps, smoking pipes and reading newspapers, or young mothers with infants sleeping under black hoods in high four-wheeled, wickerwork bassinettes.

Ten minutes stroll took us to the boating lake, deserted except for half a dozen glossy white swans and a gaggle of moor hens and mallards scrabbling for chunks of bread floating on the water. At the end of the path and, partly hidden by another high screen of rhododendron bushes, we came to Stanley Park Open Air Baths.

Being Sunday, the baths and the boating lake were closed, although this was the hottest day of a mini heat wave. However, I wasn't planning on going for a dip with the kids. I had been to Stanley Park baths, with Monty and Jackie Jones, on the previous Wednesday afternoon "Boys Only" session. "Entrance 1d. Bring your own towel". It was my first visit, and also my last, for I didn't take kindly to the rough, concrete pool, or the hordes of screeching, skinny-dipping boys, many with dirt-encrusted ankles and snotty noses, running wild in the tiny overcrowded pool. Nor to the dead leaves and empty Woodbine cigarette packets and bits of flotsam and jetsam floating on the top of the dirty looking water. Furthermore, despite the unusual hot August sun, the water was only a degree or two above freezing, as most of the pool was in the shade of overhanging trees. That Wednesday afternoon after my brief, breathtaking, initial dip in the shallow end of the murky water I had spent the rest of the permitted half-hour sitting on the cold concrete surround of the pool, guarding our clothes and boots and shivering uncontrollably.

Standing outside the entrance to the baths was a pedestal drinking fountain. One of many scattered about the parks and open spaces of Liverpool. Made of ribbed, cast iron, the fountain stood about three feet high and had a round dished-shaped bowl inset at the top. The ice-cold water bubbled out of a nozzle at the back of the basin, when you twisted one of two round control knobs each side of the basin.

The girls made a beeline for it as soon as they saw it.

"I want a drink, Doug, I want a drink. I'm thirsty. Can I have a drink from the fountain."

They weren't the only thirsty ones, for already there was a queue. When our turn came to drink I found that it was easier said than done. I was not much taller than the fountain, or, for that matter Rene and Jean. And we were all in our Sunday best. I had had strict instructions from mother that the girls were not to dirty their frocks because they were going to Sunday School that afternoon, and, also, Uncle Peter and Aunty Gertie were coming for tea.

With great difficulty, one hand wrapped around her waist, I hoisted Jean up over the top of the basin and with the other twisted the knob at the side, as she bent over the bowl to drink from the bubble of water.

Moderately successful in that the only damage to the girls' Sunday frocks was a golden stain across the front of Jean's where she had leaned over the edge of the rusty bowl, we made our way on down the path.

This, shortly, opened to an eye-catching galaxy of flowers in full bloom, bright sunshine glistening on wet leaves after their early morning watering. There were hundreds of them, neatly and precisely displayed in weed-free beds arranged in squares and circles, crescents and triangles. The dazzling display of busy lizzies, African daisies, antirrhinums, pansies, petunias and every variety of summer annuals you could think of, had all been grown from seed in the majestic dome-shaped glass Palm House in the corner overlooking the vivid display. Each bed was separated by litter free paths and guarded by the low ornamental iron railings painted a bright green. The display covered an area half the size of Liverpool or Everton's football pitch on the opposite corners of the park.

In pride-of-place in all its glory in the middle of the flower garden, was the famous Stanley Park Floral Clock. In a circular bed of massed flowers, three times the size of the front garden of 45, Waltham Road, its flower-decked hands were pointing at Roman numerals formed from more of the brilliant bedding plants.

"The fingers aren't moving", said Rene, after we had stopped in front of the six at the foot of the clock, a picture in itself made up of multi-coloured pansies and violas.

"Yes they are, Rene," I said, "Close one eye and keep very still and look at the big finger and watch it move towards the twelve."

We stood in silence as the fingers moved slowly to ten o'clock, when to the kids' delight, the cuckoo popped out from a little wooden box above the figure twelve and cuckooed ten times. Together they counted its musical performance and when it jumped back into its box, Jean said, "I'm still thirsty. Can't we go to Auntie May's now?"

Ten minutes later we knocked on the door of 18, Ince Avenue to be greeted by a strong aroma of frying bacon and eggs and, even though it was a sweltering day, a roaring fire burning up the chimney in the Living Room. The fire was to heat the water for their Sunday baths. 18 Ince Avenue was a posh house and had a bathroom with hot water heated in a boiler at the back of the fire. Auntie May, at the foot of the stairs in the narrow hallway, beads of sweat dripping from her forehead onto a flowered pinny spattered with black pudding stains, was shouting, at the top of her voice, "Come on Harry, your breakfast's ready". She was calling cousin Harry, not Uncle Harry, who she told me had gone out to his allotment and we could go and see him on our way home.

We didn't stay long at Aunty May's. Cousin Lenny was still in bed, so there was no Dandelion and Burdoch, or Sarsaparilla, for me that afternoon, and Auntie May was doing her best to get young Harry out of bed to come down for his breakfast. So she didn't have too much time for us. She and cousin Edna had already had their breakfast and Edna had gone to visit her married sister, our eldest cousin, Phyllis.

After saying our goodbyes we set off for Waltham Road and home, via Coney Green and Uncle Harry's allotment, and, hopefully, Uncle Harry. For the Arkles at the corner of Arkles Lane and Anfield Road didn't open until eleven o'clock.

The glamorously named Coney Green, was an open space bounded by Utting Avenue, Priory Road and Anfield Cemetery. For some reason or other, the field was never included as part of the Cemetery, the largest burial ground in Liverpool. It is now the site of Anfield Comprehensive School. Before the school was built Coney Green, during the summer months, hosted numerous fund-raising fetes and bazaars for local churches. Collins' travelling fun-fair regularly appeared there on their annual visit to Liverpool and one of my earliest sporting memories was of my brother, Ken, breaking the wooden ball on the coconut shy and winning a coconut for me. The top part of the field was the home in winter of St. Margaret's Amateur Football Club, and in the summer, their baseball team. The allotments occupied the lower part of the field at the top of Ince Avenue.

When we arrived on that baking Sunday morning we found Uncle Harry – an older version of my father - lying on a deck-chair, his legs sprawled, in the shade of the little garden shed which he had painstakingly made out of old plywood tea-chests and secondhand 2" x 2" roof joists. His steel-rimmed pince-nez spectacles were perched on the end of his nose and he was reading the News of the World. A large straw hat covered his balding head, and a short-stemmed black pipe with an enormous bowl big enough to take half an ounce of Ogdens' St. Julians shag tobacco was clenched between his teeth.

Uncle Harry's allotment seemed to be growing only potatoes and rhubarb, obviously aided by a heap of Mr. Sayers' manure piled up near the entrance. Red and green stalks of rhubarb, as thick as my wrist and two feet long, with gigantic leaves like elephants' ears fanning from the top, completely surrounded the plot.

He hurriedly folded up the spread-eagled News of the World and pulled his miniature incinerator out of his mouth. He said "Hello kids, has your Aunty May sent you for some rhubarb?"

I was too shy, and not cheeky enough, anyway, to reply saying, " No, I've come for my Sunday Penny". But I had no need to, for without more ado he took four pennies out of his pocket, gave us one each saying, as he usually did say 'Don't spend it all in one shop'.

Climbing out of the deck chair, Uncle Harry reached around to his back pocket and produced a large, black-handled, multi-bladed Swiss pocketknife. After demonstrating to us, once again, the use of the many blades of the knife, finishing with the one that prized stones out of horses' hooves, he said ' Come on kids, I'll give you some rhubarb to take home to your Mum'. And, repeating the joke he always cracked when he gave me rhubarb, he said 'I hope she still has that long baking tin, 'cos this rhubarb is quite a size'. Breaking off six stems of the fruit from the root, he cut off the elephant's ears with the Swiss knife and wrapped the red sticks of fruit in the faded pages of an old News of the World Sunday newspaper.

We arrived home hot and weary and hungry, just in time for Sunday dinner of roast beef and crisp, brown Yorkshire puddings, for mother had already placed the steaming tureens of roast potatoes, cabbage, and carrot and turnip on the damask covered table.

Too late for Sunday school I spent the afternoon helping her to bake rhubarb and apple tarts for Sunday tea. My job was, firstly, to remove any soil from Uncle Harry's allotment, carefully clean under very cold water and then cut the long, pale-pink and red sticks into one inch pieces, ready to be heavily sprinkled with sugar and raisins and then spread on the pastry covered plates.

Chapter 15

A Day Out Over The Water

The Arthur Family, of Waltham Road, on the blistering Monday of the August Bank Holiday heat-wave of 1928, en masse, and much against Father's inclination, came to a momentous decision to have a day-out over the water to New Brighton.

As it turned out it was more like a half day, really, for most of the morning was spent by Mother making sure that all the children were suitably attired in their Sunday Best; and then cutting up two, two-pound loaves of bread to make salmon-paste sandwiches for the family and best boiled ham sandwiches for Father.

Wrapped firstly in squares of grease-proof paper and then in back numbers of the Liverpool Echo, the sandwiches were finally wrapped in a clean white towel and packed carefully in a large, brown, leather Gladstone bag loaned by Father's life-long friend and Arkles companion-in-arms, "Uncle" Bunny Barnard, who refused, emphatically, an invitation to come along with us.

Room was also found in Mr. Gladstone's bag – or should I say "Uncle" Bunny's bag - for one of Mother's fruit bun-loaves, which she had baked especially for the occasion. The precious cake, in a Crawford's biscuit tin, was crammed in with a catering-size tin of pineapple chunks, and a bag of shelled mixed nuts by courtesy of Alf and his never ending supply of office "free samples".

A somewhat battered, four-pint, aluminium tea-pot, inside of which were two packets of connie-onnie tea mash, also went in the picnic bag with four chipped enamelled mugs, the spout of the teapot poking out of one end of the bag, as if pointing the way to New Brighton.

Tea bags yet to be invented, connie-onnie tea mash was the universal method of the day for providing a picnic brew of tea, or the tea-break on a building site, or for that matter the office or factory. The mash was made with equal measures of Nestle's, sweet, condensed milk, sugar and loose tea, mixed in a sticky mess on a square of grease-proof paper and wrapped in more pages of the aforementioned Liverpool Echo. The boiling water to brew the mash cost a thrupenny bit from one of the many tearooms and cafes dotted along the promenade at New Brighton.

But, as a concession to Mum, the founder of the feast, a tiny china teapot had also been included, just for her, with some loose tea, a carefully wrapped, white bone-china cup, and Sayers' fresh milk carried in one of Father's old McLeans Milk-of-Magnesia medicine bottles. Mother drew the line at connie-onnie tea for herself.

That morning, all the children had been through the usual weekly rigmarole of the tin bath and the nit inspection and the change of underclothes and the polishing of boots and shoes, and we were all dressed in our Sunday Best. Rene and Jean in new, flowered cotton dresses and black patent-leather shoes and red ribbons in their hair, freshly-washed after their bath that morning. Father had had a win on the horses the previous week. Hence the new dresses. Wally and I were in our customary blue and red woollen summer and winter jerseys and Ken was setting Waltham Road on fire in a sporty, brown-and-yellow check suit of plus-fours and heavy, brown and white brogues embellished with yellow stockings. The plus-fours really belonged to brother Harold who at that particular moment was starting the ascent of Snowdon on the Pyg Track, hand in hand with Helen, and was blissfully unaware of his unofficial loan to Ken of his treasured plus fours recently bought on the never-never from Newsham's, the family tailor – the "Credit Tailors of Islington". For many years afterwards, Harold and Ken still differed over who was responsible for the "loan" of Harold's fashionable, eye-catching plus fours and who was responsible for the shilling-size cigarette burn in the baggy trousers!

"The Old Man" with complete disregard for the now intense heat, was in his customary blue serge single-breasted three-piece suit, a heavy silver watch-chain glinting in the sun looped across the fob pockets of his waistcoat, highly polished black boots and a brilliant-white, stiff celluloid collar, one of the six I had collected from the opium den the day before. His bowler hat had been brushed immaculately with the special brush from the hat stand. Father never wore anything else but a blue serge suit and a bowler hat, even when he went to work as a plumber.

The morning was almost over before we set out, Father, Mother, Alf, Ken, myself, Wally, Rene and Jean. Harold was the only absentee, having gone Youth Hostelling and climbing Snowdon with his new girl friend, Helen. The Youth Hostels Association had been formed that year.

By now the sun, blazing down right overhead from a bright blue, cloudless sky had melted the tar in the granite sets of Waltham Road forming hot, squelchy bubbles in the joints. We hadn't gone more than ten yards when Wally broke away from the party, squatted on his haunches on the kerb at the side of the road and, before anyone could twig what he was up to, poked his fingers in the miniature, volcano-like eruptions of black tar. In a matter of seconds his hand was covered in hot tar and amid explosive remonstrations. " What did you do that for? And you're in your Sunday Best. Keep your hands off your jersey and do you want to stay at home by yourself then and play with the tar?" We all did an about face and trooped back to No. 45.

Ever resourceful, mother took a half-pound packet of margarine out of the meat safe in the back kitchen to clean the tar on Wally's hands, changed his woollen jersey, told him not to be such a stupid boy, and ten minutes later we made a second attempt to go to New Brighton.

It was a short walk to the No. 13 and No. 14 tram-stop at Cabbage Hall, the junction of Priory Road, Lower Breck Road and Townsend Lane and a turning point for trams not going on to Norris Green and Gill Moss. And there was a perspiring queue of fifty or sixty would-be day-trippers when we got there, half of them under the age of five. The queue was moving slowly but surely on to a No. 13 and there were two more trams waiting to make the turn round at the junction. One of them moved onto the single track in Townsend Lane and I watched the driver as he pulled down the trolley arm from the overhead electric cable and drag it to the reverse end of the tram, magically making the back-end of the tram the front and what was the front, the back. The destination sign on the front now said PIER HEAD via Islington, so we knew we were really on our way, at last.

I began to get a little worried though when the driver seemed to be having difficulty in getting the wheel of the trolley arm to fit on the overhead cable, each attempt slipping off and sparks flying like flashes from a rip-rap on bon-fire night. Successful on the fourth attempt he made fast the trolley arm rope onto a hook above his head on the platform and then walked through the "inside" of the tram from what was now the rear, to the front, reversing the back rests of the wooden seats as he did so, to face the right way. The antediluvian tram was one of the Liverpool Passenger Transport's famous "bone-shakers" later to be replaced by the luxurious "Green Goddesses".

When our turn came to board, the Arthur Family, not for the last time on that adventurous day-out, was split into three parties. Mother, with the two girls and Wally went inside the lower deck. **NO SMOKING** and

STANDING ROOM for 12 ONLY painted in black letters over the sliding door entrance. Inside, was the lower deck, between the two end platforms, with two long, plywood-faced benches facing each other down the sides of the tram, under the windows. Above the seating arrangement, a line of leather loops hanging from the ceiling was for the benefit of the Standing Room Only passengers. A broad, black leather strap running down the middle of the ceiling from each end operated the bell above the driver's head. The conductor pulled it once to tell the driver when a passenger wanted to get off at the next stop, or twice to tell the driver he could proceed after picking up another passenger.

Alf, who had been carrying the Gladstone bag, was more than pleased to leave it in the limited luggage space under the short spiral staircase to the upper deck, where it was immediately buried under a miniature mountain of assorted picnic hampers, ex-army haversacks, threadbare rucksacks, leather brief cases and a home made canvas holdall with two child's buckets and spades tied to the outside, all heading for New Brighton. Dad, Alf, Ken and I climbed to the upper deck. Another notice in heavy black letters was over the door, **STRICTLY NO STANDING ALLOWED**. Father and Alf went in, lighting up their Capstan Medium Strength cigarettes almost before they sat down.

Ken and I found seats in, to me, the most exciting section of the tram, the half round cage in the open air at the front of the Upper Deck. Ken, defying the **NO SMOKING** signs on the stairs and the strict instructions from Father, surreptitiously lighting his fourth cigarette of the day and keeping it cupped behind his hand. From this exciting vantage point, I could watch the driver at the foot of the spiral stairs, operating with a circular motion the two brass handles to drive the tram, his left hand controlling the speed and his right hand operating the brakes. By his foot was an iron disc recessed in the floor, which he stamped on, violently, to sound a warning bell with a "clang-clang-clang-clangity-clang" whenever he approached an intersection or saw a dog on the tramlines

The tram was packed to overflowing when we eventually got going and inside the "Standing Room for 12 only" sign had been ignored completely. For after the normal courtesies of the day had been carried out by most of the male passengers, who vacated their seats to allow the ladies to sit down, it was packed, shoulder to shoulder, with a miscellaneous assortment of red-faced, perspiring standing passengers, only the fortunate twelve hanging grimly onto the leather loops. Jammed together, like sardines in a tin, a strong aroma of the unwashed bodies of those who had failed to use the tin bath that morning, mixed with bursts of Californian Poppy – a popular scent used by young ladies at that time - wafted freely, through the car, from front to back. Even the Conductor's platform was crammed with day-outers, despite another black painted warning sign that passengers were not allowed to travel on the platform nor to engage in conversation with the conductor.

The poor, harassed conductor, sweat running down his cheeks from under his Liverpool Corporation Tramways peaked cap, was clad in the regulation heavy blue serge Liverpool Corporation Tramways uniform. Slung over one shoulder he carried a capacious leather money satchel and over the other, a ticket machine holding a selection of brightly coloured cardboard tickets. A metal punch clipped to his belt completed his tools of the trade. Announcing his presence to the crowded compartment by repeatedly shaking the copper coins in his moneybag and calling "Fares, please, fares please, have your fares ready please, fares please", he was forcing his way through the melee collecting the fares. Twopence for adults, a penny for children under fourteen and free if a child sat on the knee of a parent. On payment he handed over a white ticket, after punching a hole in one corner. It was remarkable how many of the fourteen-year-olds and fifteen-year-olds, even little sixteen-year-olds, were sitting on their mother's knee!

The conductor had put the "chain" across the entrance, indicating that the tram was full and, as everyone was going to the Pier Head, it was not going to stop for anyone. The driver set off like a bat out of hell without stopping at any of the official stops.

To a nine-year-old the crazy, buffeting ride on the bone-shaker was as thrilling and exciting as a ride on the expensive, death-defying "High Flier" of Wallis's World Famous Travelling Fun-Fair on its annual visit to Cherry Lane. At any speed over about ten miles per hour, the tram's short four-wheeled bogie set the antediluvian bone-shaker rocking, or shaddling, violently from side to side and corner to corner like a more dangerous version of the American Cake-Walk, also one of Wallis's major attractions. But the thrilling climax of the whole trip, for me, was reached when the ancient tram careered to a vibrating halt over Everton Brow at the top of Fitzclarence Street. There it had to wait because a No. 14 tram was already making its way down the steep incline to Shaw Street and the City. The obligatory halt was to prevent a repeat of a recent minor disaster when, half way down the hill, the brakes on a No. 14 failed completely and had caught up with and then crashed into a No. 13 which was still making its careful way down.

From my seat in the open-air cage on the top deck at the front of the tram, with the sun beating down from a bright clear blue sky, the short halt enabled me to take in the spectacular panoramic view of the City of Liverpool and the distant River Mersey. The everyday smoke-laden fog from the city's countless chimneys was noticeably absent and I could see, highlighted by the colourful rolling background of the Clwydian Hills in North Wales, and the pimple on the top of Moel Fammau, the Liver Building, the Cunard Building and the Port of Liverpool Building – "The Three Graces" – at the Pier Head. And I could just make out, at the mouth of the river the square, red brick buildings of New Brighton Ballroom framed against a backdrop of the Great Orme at Llandudno, and beyond that, the feint outlines of the Isle of Anglesey. And I could hardly contain my excitement when I spotted grey-black smoke streaming from the funnel of a ferry on its way to Seacombe and New Brighton, and the North Wales pleasure steamer, *St. Tudno*, on its afternoon trip to Llandudno and Anglesey. I promised myself there and then that I was going to be a sailor when I left school.

The No. 13, after safely negotiating the incline down Fitzclarence Street, passed the doss houses of Shaw Street and turned right into Islington. The City centre was almost deserted of traffic except for the lines of trams making their way to and from the Pier Head, which we joined in Dale Street. The lumbering trams trundled from every suburb of Liverpool to the Pier Head, for the routes from the Pier Head's three circular tram terminuses spread out, fanlike, to Speke and Garston, Woolton and Bowring Park, Norris Green and Gill Moss and Seaforth Sands and Crosby. In fact you could find your way on the tram to any district in Liverpool by making your way, firstly, to the Pier Head.

When we finally arrived there - the clocks under the Liver Bird telling us it was now nearly twelve o'clock - excitedly we piled off the tram with frequent exhortations from Father to " All keep together now. Don't go wandering off on your own. Alf, hold on to our Wally's hand" and "Ken, keep that little bugger, Doug, away from the chains at the side". And in the company of hundreds of other eager day-trippers, the Arthur Family tagged on to the end of yet another queue making its way down the steep slope of the open floating gangway to the ferries at the Landing Stage.

The floating gangway was used normally for road traffic – mainly horse drawn carts and drays pulled by teams of two or four and sometimes six gigantic Shire horses - from the commercial ferries crossing the river. It was a floating roadway moored between the river wall and the landing stage, with walkways each side flanked by two linked safety chains looped to iron stanchions to prevent runaway children from falling into the fast flowing murky waters of the River Mersey. The swiftly racing tide was on the ebb and the floating roadway sloped steeply down to the landing stage at an alarming angle, the huge hawsers and chains anchoring the stage to the green, algae covered wall of the river, hanging free from the water and festooned with trails of slimy seaweed, discarded clothes, scraps of newspapers and flotsam and jetsam of all kinds.

By the look of it, too, the *Ulster Prince*, or one of the many Irish coasters on the Liverpool – Dublin - Belfast sailing, had unloaded a cargo of cattle early that morning, for the animals on the way to Stanley abattoir, had left their unmistakable trade-mark in the roadway. The cow pancakes had been trodden on and spread by the shoes of the New Brighton bound trippers, bringing more instructions from Father to "Look where you're going now, be careful, mind your new shoes girls, don't walk in the muck".

Vessels of all types and sizes were bustling about the river; flimsy, one-man yachts, keeling over in the breeze tossed and turned alarmingly in the wakes of passing ferries; tramp steamers in dire need of a coat of paint edging their way in and out of the line of docks alongside the Overhead Railway; the *Ben McCrie*, an Isle of Man Steam Packet ferry, tied up at the landing stage embarking passengers for the Island; and the pride of Liverpool's Cunard Steamship Co., the majestic, immaculate four-funnel liner, *Mauritania*, just leaving the stage on its regular sailing to New York making its way, shepherded fore and aft by two tug-boats, to the mouth of the river.

Alf, who had worked in a shipping office in Liverpool since leaving school was an encyclopaedia of knowledge about the river and the shipping and the docks, and could name the many shipping lines by the house colours on the funnels of the vessels. He pointed out

117

to me ships belonging to The White Star Line and the Cunard Steamship Company, the Blue Funnel Line and Coast Lines, owners of ships leaving the Port of Liverpool, every day, bound to all points of the globe. The towering Mammoth Crane, the largest floating crane in the world, was making slow progress across the Mersey to Cammell Llaird's shipyard in Birkenhead, and the "Liverpool Hopper", a sand-dredger with its endless chain of huge buckets clearing silt from the bed of the river. Alf pointed out the two Royal Navy training ships, the renowned *Conway* and *Indefatigable* anchored permanently in the Mersey at New Ferry. One was for ordinary seamen and the other for commissioned officers.

"That would be the life for me", I thought and asked Alf if I could put my name down. *"You'll have to wait until you leave school"*, he said, *"But don't tell Father"*. On that busy, beautiful August Monday Bank Holiday, when the whole of Liverpool seemed to heading for a "day out across the water", the vehicle ferries were out to help the passenger ferries to carry the day-trippers to the five landing stages of the Wirral peninsula. Rock Ferry, Birkenhead, Seacombe, Egremont and New Brighton. The ferries' foaming wakes glistened in the sunshine and made constantly changing patterns as they plied to and fro across the water, foghorns sounding a distant, friendly, holiday hullabaloo as they passed each other, their funnels leaving clouds of black smoke drifting on the water.

We came to a halt on the landing stage just in time to watch the Mersey ferry, the *Royal Daffodil*, a naval veteran of the first world war, manoeuvring into its berth to take on another load of passengers. Separated from the river by about six foot of landing stage and the single safety chain looped across, I could feel under my feet the vibrations of the ferry's propellers. I watched, fascinated, as the huge screws, with intermittent bursts of power, churned the water into a vast bubbling, seething, frothing witches cauldron, as they slowly edged the ferry

into its allotted position.   Alf pointed out to me that its
movements were controlled by the Captain whose peaked
cap I could just see in his cabin on the upper deck at the
side of the ferry.

In front of me, alongside a massive iron bollard set
into the edge of the landing stage, a weather-beaten,
peaked-capped sailor wearing a dark blue, polo-necked
jersey, emblazoned with the words "Mersey Ferries" across
the chest, stood ready to catch a coil of rope from a deck
hand standing by two bollards under the taffrail at the
stern of the ferry. As the screws ceased their rumbling
in the water, the *Daffodil* edged alongside the stage with
scarcely a bump and the deck hand deftly threw the rope
to the waiting sailor. Attached to it was a loop of a two-
inch thick heavy manila hawser, which he quickly pulled
in and threw over the bollard.   Simultaneously, with
amazing dexterity and speed, the deck hand on the ferry
threw the other end of the rope across the two bollards
winding it around them like a figure of eight. The hawser,
creaking and protesting loudly, took the strain as the tide
attempted to carry the boat away from the stage. the *Royal
Daffodil* was safely moored to the landing stage ready to
take on more passengers for the trip to New Brighton,
including, hopefully, the Arthur Family.

The   impatient   waiting   day-trippers,   all   visibly
affected by the overhead heat of the sun, surged forward
to board the ferry via two gangways lowered from the
landing stage, like drawbridges lowered over a swiftly
flowing castle moat, onto the decks of the gently rocking
ferry, one to the lower deck and one, via a short flight
of stairs, to the upper deck.   The Arthur Family, with
Father sweating heavily in his blue serge suit and hard
bowler hat and issuing loud vocal instructions again that
"Everybody keep together now, but if you get separated
make for the main lounge on the lower deck".   Whether
we liked it or not, we were carried forward by the press
of the impatient queue, eager to seek the fresh air of the
open deck and, in my case, to experience the thrill of my

first ocean going voyage.

Ken took a firm grip of my hand and said, "Hold on to me Doug, we'll find the others later, after we've got ourselves a good spec."

Once across the drawbridge, the patient, good-natured crowd spread out to all parts of the ferry, as did the Arthur Family. Father and Mother with the two girls and Wally, found seats in the glass-covered smoker's Lounge and Alf, who had met a business acquaintance, stood chatting and smoking on the crowded top-deck.

Ken, with me in tow almost unable to contain my excitement, explored the *Royal Daffodil* from stem to stern, including the smelly urinals somewhere down in the bowels of the ship. We reached the top deck just in time to see a silver and black, two-winged aeroplane trundling along almost overhead. It was pulling a long advertising drogue highlighted in huge red letters with a message from Lord Leverhulme. **LEVERS SUNLIGHT SOAP.** And as I looked skywards, I saw a puff of steam spurt from the top of the funnel, followed by a double blast from the foghorn almost making me jump out of my skin, as we passed across the bow of the *Royal Iris* making its way to the berth on the landing stage we had just vacated.

Our exploration of the *Daffodil* came to a halt at the top of a hatchway leading down into the engine room. A chain was strung across the top of the stairs from which hung a notice. **"Engine Room. Entrance Strictly Forbidden. Crew only."** As I leaned over the rail the steady, regular throb of the engines was more pronounced and a blast of hot air reeking of oil and what I took to be some of Mother's Brasso cleaning polish swept across my face. At the bottom of the immaculately white painted stairs a maze of highly polished copper pipes was running along the wall and I could just see the end of a huge piston moving slowly but regularly, up and down.

My gawking ceased abruptly when a sailor came bounding up the stairs pulling a packet of cigarettes out of his trousers pocket. He was wearing a black peaked cap pushed to the back of his head and his lined, red face was running with sweat. His white trousers and singlet were grubby and stained with black oil and the dirty rag he used to swab the sweat off his face was not much cleaner, either. I changed my mind, there and then, about joining the Navy as a boy recruit!

The throbbing of the engine beneath my feet suddenly altered its tempo and I turned to see that we were approaching Seacombe. Five minutes later the *Daffodil* bumped lightly against the landing stage at the end of the pier, and two deckhands, with slick co-operation, again secured the ferry to the pier with the thick hawsers.

The two narrow strips of sand each side of Seacombe pier were packed with trippers and I couldn't see how the few passengers getting off the ferry would find space.

Fifteen minutes later we were tying up at New Brighton pier and I wanted to know from Ken if we would see the One-Legged-Diver. I had heard all about the famous diver with only one leg making his perilous dive off the end of New Brighton pier, and Tommy Handley's equally famous catch phrase "Don't forget the diver". But Ken said he wouldn't be there today because the tide was out and if he dived he'd only break his neck. So I never got to see New Brighton's One-Legged-Diver, although later on, I did see his dare-devil act reproduced at Wallis's Fun Fair in Cherry Lane by a diver diving off a high-level platform into a six-foot diameter, six-foot high, water tank.

We joined the crowd walking along the promenade, reluctantly passing by the candy-floss stalls and the photographer's booths and the fish-and-chip shops and the indoor children's fun-fair near the Floral Pavilion Theatre, until Father saw a vacant spot on the crowded beach near the Perch Rock Lighthouse.

After collecting a folding canvas deck chair for Mother – hired for the day for sixpence from a long stack of chairs on the promenade, guarded by a man in a brown smock – we carefully made our way down the steep slippery, seaweed strewn sandstone stairs from the promenade, under strict instructions from Father to "Now look where you're going, don't slip on the seaweed and mind that pool of water at the bottom, it'll ruin those new shoes", we finally made it to the overcrowded, rock-strewn, slightly muddy beach of New Brighton.

At the tiny island of sand in the middle of the crowded beach, Father gave us all further instructions on how to locate our patch of sand should we get lost when we went looking for crabs in the rock pools around the lighthouse or, in his case, when he went to the pub on the promenade.

"Now don't go wandering off and get lost. And if you do, take a bearing from that high lamppost by the side of the toilets on the promenade", he said, like a three-striper on an Artillery Observation Post, "And line it up with the middle of the Lighthouse. And then walk down the line". Rene and Jean looked in vain for the line and decided to stay put, near Mother.

There was just about enough space for us, on our newly won patch of sand, alongside a very friendly family who, it turned out, were on a week's holiday from Sheffield. They spoke with a very strange accent, which could have been Chinese as far as we children were concerned, but Father could interpret quite well for he had been attached to a Sheffield Artillery Regiment during the First World War. They budged over a bit so that there was room for him to erect Mother's deck chair, swearing quietly under his breath after he had twice caught his fingers in the complicated folding woodwork mechanism. Gratefully, Mother sat down on the chair and The Arthur Family gathered in a circle around it as Dad said, "Where's the Gladstone bag? Put it under the chair until we're ready for something to eat." .

At that moment the eight of us were smitten, as they say, with a deathly silence, broken only by the background of shrill children's voices on the beach, and the feint swishing of the tide against the wall of the Perch Rock

Lighthouse, and the distant lazy drone of the Sunlight Soap message making its way back in the skies over the River Mersey.

The Gladstone Bag!

Where was it?

What's happened to the Gladstone Bag?

Where were the salmon paste sandwiches, and the tin of pears, and the precious connie-onnie tea mash? Not to mention the mixed nuts and the bunloaf.

But the Gladstone Bag was conspicuous by its very absence.

I was permanently hungry in those days, and for that matter for many days and months afterwards, but on that day, the New Brighton ozone had put a further razor edge to my appetite and my empty stomach was rumbling. So my heart dropped when I realized the bag was missing and I said to myself " What are we going to do for something to eat?" I had visions of starving to death on New Brighton Beach.

And then I was struck with a bright thought. "Of course we'll have to have chips, even if it's only half a portion. It would be better than salmon-paste sandwiches, anyway". I quickly realized, however, that chips was a non-starter for a family of eight hungry Arthurs. I had been sent for chips, many a time, to Metcalf's chippie in Townsend Lane and knew their cost only too well.

The unusual, brief Arthur silence was broken suddenly when we all started talking at once and Jean had burst into tears.

"Where's the Gladstone Bag?" Father said, his voice rising to a crescendo and causing our new Sheffield friends to cease their Mandarin chatter. "Where's the bag. Where's the bloody bag, Alf?" And Father seldom swore in front of the children or raised his voice in public.

"Ken, where's the bloody bag? You were supposed to be looking after the bag. The plus-fours must have gone to your head you silly bugger, you've left the bag on the tram."

He took off his bowler hat and mopped his balding head with the white handkerchief from his top pocket and, unusual for him, sat down in his Best Suit on the damp sand alongside Mother's deck chair.

Alf, as usual, poured oil on the troubled waters of the Arthur family, stepping into the breach saying, "Yes we've left it on the tram. I'll go back. The conductor will have probably put it in the left-luggage office at the Pier Head. There's a ferry coming in, now. If I catch that I should be back in an hour or so. Father, buy the kids an ice-cream while they're waiting."

And he was off, picking his way through the crowded families and the rock pools, and dodging the strings of flying kites on the beach, back to the promenade and the ferry.

After buying the four children an ice cream from a Walls Stop-me-and-buy-one trike on the promenade, Dad was also off. Telling Mother that he had promised to meet Bunny Barnard at the Victoria pub on the corner of Victoria Road and the promenade near the ferry. "I'm only going to have a pint", he said, "I won't be long. I'll be back before Alf gets back with the bag." Mother didn't seem to mind, although she knew the pint would be at least two and probably three. She'd brought with her one of her favourite books, "Sorrell and Son", and her knitting. Father had left his News Chronicle with her and she was already in animated conversation with her opposite number from Sheffield.

Ken also was off. He had arranged to meet his new girl friend, Jean Olden, who's brother, Ted Ray was making a name for himself with his "Fiddlin' and Foolin'" act on the variety stage and was appearing that week at the Floral Pavilion in New Brighton. Jean had two tickets for the afternoon matinee.

The family didn't meet Jean that day, and it was some time before she was introduced to the family and eventually became a most welcome addition to the Arthurs after she and Ken married. I was to discover that she worked in Gallacher's sweet shop at the top of Douglas Road opposite my school. Whenever I could save or scrounge a ha'penny for sweets, I would go to Gallachers with one of my pals to swank about the lovely girl behind the counter who was "going out with our Ken".

Alf got back from the Lost Property office in Liverpool, thankfully carrying the Gladstone bag, long before Father returned from his two pints. The now slightly warm salmon paste sandwiches went down a treat, as did the fruit bun-loaf. All washed down with freshly made tea from the connie-onnie mix and boiling water from a tea-room on the promenade. But we found ourselves in another crisis when it was realized that we had forgotten to put a tin opener in the bag to open the tin of pineapple chunks. Help was at hand, though, for our new-found friends from Sheffield lent us one of those multi-bladed Swiss knives, which included a tin-opener. So the now lukewarm pineapple chunks also went down a treat.

It was shortly after we had demolished the contents of the bag, and Father had returned from the pub, that a veil was drawn over the Arthur Family's day out over the water in the shape of a menacing bank of black/grey cloud heading swiftly for New Brighton from the direction of the North Wales mountains.

We just beat the mass exodus from the beach and caught the next ferry back to Liverpool and were the first family to board an empty No. 14 tram waiting at the Pier Head. A little more than an hour after leaving New Brighton we were back at No. 45 Waltham Road and Mum was frying bubble-and-squeak for tea.

Father, unpacking the Gladstone bag to give back to "Uncle" Bunny, said, "We won't be going to New Brighton again in a hurry, our next day out will be Crosby or Formby beach. It's nearer and won't be so crowded."

Chapter 16

Farewell To 45 Waltham Road

Early in January 1929, Father received yet another notification from the Liverpool Corporation Housing Department that the long awaited tenancy of a "Corporation House" had become available for the Arthur Family.

Although the younger end of the family had not been consulted about the proposed move to "a bigger house" I was fully aware that we were going to live somewhere else for I had been with Mum on a number of occasions to look at houses in the Clubmoor, Lisburn Park and Norris Green housing estates. All of them had been turned down for various reasons. It was a "kitchen house", i.e. it didn't have a parlour, and the bedrooms were too small; the garden was too big; the garden was too small; it was too far from the tram-stop and the younger ones wouldn't be able to go to Anfield Road School anyway. Father, Alf, Harold and Ken had all been pupils of Anfield Road and it was essential that Wally and I should keep to the tradition. It was too awkward for Father to get to Walton Hospital where he worked as a plumber for he'd have to get up in the middle of the night! And, although it was never actually voiced by Father, it was too far from the "Arkles" for his occasional conferences with Uncle Harry and his close companion, Bunny Barnard.

So it was a great relief for Mother when it was decided that they should accept the offer of a tenancy of 26

Vanbrugh Crescent, a "parlour" house on the Pinehurst Avenue Estate. Why it was an essential we have a "parlour" house was lost on me, for there was never any furniture in the parlour of Waltham Road, except a dusty aspidistra standing on a rickety table.

I had mixed feelings about the move. I would have to leave all my friends, or make the twenty-minute walk up Townsend Lane each time I wanted to play out. The inconveniences of 45 Waltham Road had never bothered me. I was fully accustomed to the freezing cold weather of mid-winter, and the ice freezing the flushing cistern in the backyard, despite Father's efforts at lagging the pipe-work. The sub-zero temperature of my bedroom never bothered me, providing Alf came to bed reasonably early with his socks on, and I was always intrigued by the myriad patterns of frost on the bedroom window. Even the water-logged back-kitchen on washdays didn't bother me too much, providing Mum's thick pea-soup was available for tea.

And since the age of about seven, when I had had my tonsils out, I had kept in good health in Waltham Road like most of the other kids. True, I had had chicken-pox, measles, worms, impetigo, sore throats, stomach-upsets - you must have eaten something - and I had spent my fourth birthday in the middle of a three week stay in the "fever hospital" with scarlet fever. But all that seemed to be in the past and to me didn't seem to mean a move away from friends I had known since I could walk.

However, on my first visit with Mum to help her to measure the windows for the curtains, I had to hold up the tape, I took to 26 Vanbrugh Crescent right away. My eyes accustomed to the whitewashed walls of the narrow back yard of Waltham Road and the grey slate roofs of the houses in Winchester Road, the long back garden of the "new House" stretching to the rear of Vanbrugh Road, looked like an open field in "the country". And I had visions of Dad and my older brothers cultivating it so the Arthur family could grow their own vegetables like some of the tiny plots in the back yards of the terraced houses of Townsend Lane. I was overwhelmed with the novelty of the toilet in its own little room next to the bathroom and kept finding excuses to run up stairs to use it and pull the brass chain hanging from the lever of the cistern. I asked Mum if I could have a bath in the huge white porcelain bath with the taps in the side before we went home.

"No", she said. "The water's cold. The fire in the living room has to be lit to warm the tank up. And on Saturday, when we move in, I want you to come down with Wally and light the fire and have the house warm for when the removal van arrives. And you and Wally can have a bath on Saturday night before you go to bed. Do you think you'll be able to manage that?"

"Moving day", on the third Saturday of January was the coldest of that freezing winter and I left Waltham Road for the last time just as a removal van arrived. A small pantechnicon, Father called it. I was the proud bearer of a "grown-up" Yale key for our "new House". It was wrapped up in a handkerchief and burning a hole in my trousers pocket. Holding on to Wally with one hand, and in the other, a bucket containing a box of "Vesta" matches, an old Liverpool Echo and two bundles of dry firewood, I set off down Townsend Lane to light the fire. Mum had already had the coal delivered to the "coal-hole" in the back kitchen.

We arrived at No. 26 in a minor blizzard for it had started to snow and the wind was gusting the snow in whirls and eddies across the open space at the end of Pinehurst Avenue. Thankfully, after the twenty minutes walk down Townsend Lane, I plonked the bucket on the doorstep and fished out of my pocket the handkerchief wrapped round the key to future happiness, immediate warmth, hot baths and the bacon and egg which Mother said we could have for dinner. Wally had started to cry with the cold and wanted to know "When's me Mum coming, when will they be here?"

Standing on tiptoe I could just about reach the Yale
lock, high up on the door above the letter-box, and was
able to slide the key inside. I turned it to the right, as
instructed by Mother, (and Father and Alf and Harold
and Ken), but nothing happened. The door wouldn't
open. The door wouldn't open because the key didn't
turn. To a chorus of howls from Wally, I took the key out
of the door, wet it on my tongue, and standing on a brick
I found under the privet hedge, tried again. It was of no
avail. The key wouldn't turn and the door failed to open.

At that point, my struggles with the key were
interrupted by a pleasant voice at my back saying in a
strange accent I didn't recognize, "Give me the key, son,
I'll have a try for you." It was Mrs McCuish, an elderly
neighbour from opposite who had seen my desperate
struggles with the key as she was cleaning her windows.
The key wouldn't work for her either, so she went back to
her house returning with two more Yale keys, which also
failed to open the door.

"I'm sorry, son", she said, "They wont open. I'm
afraid you'll have to go back home and tell your Mum. It
could be some time before they get down here with the
furniture. Anyway, what do they call you? If you're going
to live opposite me, I'll need to know your name."

"Douglas", I replied. "And this is Walter, only we call
him Wally. And he's crying because he's cold".

We got back to Waltham Road just in time to see
the removal man, who had just dropped the aspidistra
pot and was trying to put the pieces together under the
beetling eyebrows of Father, who was saying, "Why the
hell can't you be more careful".

I stayed long enough to eat two thick rounds of toast
toasted by Mother on the embers of the still burning fire
in the combination grate, plastered liberally with bacon
fat and washed down with a mug of scalding Oxo.

I returned to Vanbrugh Crescent this time with Ken,
who had got home early from work to help with the move.
At the end of Winchester Road we met Les Jones who had

just pinched two King Edward potatoes from the basket outside Ashtons.

"These are for the bonny, Doug", he said. "I'm just going up there to light it. Are you coming up"

"No, Les", I replied. "I can't stop. We're moving to a house with a smashing bathroom and I'm going down to light the fire to heat the water. I can't stop."